S0-AIS-293

The Bible On Paradise

The Bible

ST. JOSEPH'S UNIVERSITY
BS680.P32H47   STX
The Bible on paradise.

3 9353 00005 4096

on

Paradise

BS
680
P32
H47

by B. HEMELSOET

Translated by F. VANDER HEIJDEN

ST. NORBERT ABBEY PRESS
De Pere, Wisconsin
U. S. A.
1965

110710

Biblical quotations are from the Revised Standard Version of the Bible, copyrighted 1946 and 1952 by the Division of Christian Education, National Council of Churches, and used by permission.

Nihil obstat:

      Samuel D. Jadin, O. Praem.
      Censor deputatus

Imprimatur:

      †Stanislaus V. Bona, D.D.
      Bishop of Green Bay
      November 30, 1965

The *Nihil obstat* and *Imprimatur* are a declaration that a book or pamphlet is considered free from doctrinal or moral error. It is not implied that those who have granted the *Nihil obstat* and *Imprimatur* agree with the contents, opinions or statements expressed.

© 1965 ST. NORBERT ABBEY PRESS

Originally published as
De Bijbel over het Paradijs
Roermond and Maaseik, J. J. Romen & Zonen, 1961

Library of Congress catalogue card number: 65 - 29093

Printed in the United States of America
ST. NORBERT ABBEY PRESS
De Pere, Wisconsin

CONTENTS

PREFACE

Speaking about paradise has become difficult in our days. There has been a veritable conspiracy on the part of those who think along the lines of the natural sciences to disregard all those dream-gardens of early humanity. All those old stories have been unmasked ("demythologized") and proved to be no more than pure phantasies, having no relation to historical facts.

A difficulty lies in the fact that we are inclined to keep asking ourselves what really and exactly happened. We like to look at the biblical story of paradise as at a historical account of the past. We cannot help feeling exactly as the Jew of the legend does: seeing the autumn leaves falling from the trees and the storm clouds sweep over the land, he concludes that paradise cannot yet have been restored, the Messiah has not yet come.

Indeed, if we ask ourselves what it was that really happened to the first human beings, the account of the first pages of Genesis hardly stand a chance to be taken seriously. The dream-garden we read about there, with its wonder-trees and its sly serpent, have nothing in common with the world we live in or with the animals and trees we find around us. The conclusion seems obvious: the biblical story has no scientific value and consequently

has no existential value for us today. We need pay no
more attention to it than we pay to any of those texts
we find on potsherds of olden times. At best we
can appreciate them as interesting examples of the
age-old endeavors to put into words certain indes-
tructible longings of the human heart.

Indeed, if the paradise of the Bible were just one
of those stories, such a verdict would be justified.
But it is not just one of those stories. It is not even
a story standing by itself. It is not lying before us
like one of those museum pieces behind protecting
glass, a rarity with a clarifying label. This story is
the very first story of the Bible. It is the glorious
gateway through which we pass in order to reach
the wide domain of the holy books. It is part and
parcel of the great mystery which is contained in
holy Scripture. These opening chapters of the Bible
must be governed by the principle that binds together all the books that make up the Bible: the
principle, that is, that Jesus has risen from death
and is sitting now at the right hand of his heavenly
Father, and that we are sharing in their Spirit.
Looked at in this way, the paradise story becomes
part of that great mystery to which it testifies in its
own way: the mystery of our redemption in the name
of the Father and of the Son and of the Holy Spirit.
It is in the first place a testimony to the Father.

This is what the story of paradise purports to be.
Only after having thoroughly convinced ourselves
of this may we venture to ask whether this story

too perhaps has something in common with the
human dreams of centuries ago — something found
on the potsherds.

Paradise and its story are a part of holy Scripture.
As such it too comes under the general injunction of
Jesus: "Search the scriptures . . . it is they that bear
witness to me" (John 5, 39).

This, I think, is what enlightens our understanding
of paradise. The very first thing we must look for
is testimony about our salvation. The very first
thing we want to read in it is what God is like and
how he wants to deal with us.

1

CONDITIONS FOR UNDERSTANDING PARADISE

We are going to deal with the question about paradise in the holy books. But this is more than simply the question about the wonder-garden of the first chapters of Genesis: We want to lift these chapters above their own context and consider them above all as moments in the great movement of God, as signs of the great testimony of the Scriptures: the Lord has risen! We want to investigate how paradise — whether on the first pages of holy Scripture or not — plays its part in the testimony of the holy books about the wonderful work of Redemption. We want to investigate how the imagery of paradise plays a part in the presentation of the great works of God, and not only on the threshold of holy Scripture. We want to investigate what Scripture says and what its testimony has to tell us about what the Lord did in paradise.

We therefore ask ourselves how the idea of a sacred enclosure plays a part throughout the Scriptures. We want to know what Scripture means when it speaks about an enclosed garden, where God is Lord and Master, where he wants to be together with man,

and why jewels and great rivers confer to its abundant wealth: why there should be a garden planted
by God. We want to know why Scripture represents
God as arranging a place where he approaches man
and desires to be intimate with him.

Meditating in this way about paradise and about
the holy Garden, it becomes evident that according
to holy Scripture itself we must comply with certain
conditions, which show us the way toward a possible
solution and which can help us to understand the
story of a place which God arranged for our glory.

The very **first condition** — and this holds good for
every question of holy Scripture — is: we must realize that God himself is the first and last subject of
the holy books. They start with "In the beginning,"
because at that moment God creates heaven and
earth. And they finish when the mysterious revelation of St. John is completed: "the grace of Jesus
Christ" is the conclusion of the books.

This is more than only interesting; it is highly significant, because it shows us that holy Scripture
grows from God toward Jesus; that the intimacy
which God wants to bring about with us becomes
more and more pronounced; that its meaning becomes
more and more clear; that the crowning clearness
comes in Jesus, who is Emmanuel, which is God-with-
us.

This we must always remember: everything in the
Scriptures revolves first of all around God, who

makes himself known by acting among us, by wanting to be with us.

God can act among us in two ways. He can come to us for our salvation and sanctification. He can also come in punishing judgment. His action can be for the fall as well as for the rise of man, for his curse, as well as for his blessing. There exists a paradisic blessing as well as a paradisic curse.

God's saving activity in paradise tells us — judging from the stories of holy Scripture — three things.

1. God's action arranges a place, that is to say, a holy place; his action changes the place where he appears. There where he touches the world, something happens, a change takes place. And where something is changed, there is his domain; there he draws the confines of his peculiar property.

We know the place where he acted. We can point it out in this world, and people can make note of it. The mountains emit smoke when God shakes them, and when the water of Cana reflects the face of our Lord it blushes for royal pleasure.

A bush burns with a strange glow and it is not consumed. Moses approaches hesitatingly and is bidden to take off his shoes, because the place where he stands is holy. In that mysterious fire God speaks, in that wonderful event God is near; nature holds it breath, as it always does when God visits the world.

Jacob has a dream. A ladder is let down from

heaven; angels come down and go up: the approach
to the divine dwelling place is revealed. To mark
this, Jacob anoints a stone; thus he indicates that
this is a stone which is different from other stones
roundabout. Above this stone the heavens have
opened; from this stone contact with heaven is
assured.

God appears to Abraham, and this prince of
patriarchs builds an altar in the place where the
Lord has appeared to him. The altar is a beacon, a
sign which marks a place which belongs to the Lord
and protects it in such a way that contact with the
world above shall not be lost.

Where God acts, the world changes, and people
to whom this is made known recognize this. They
build an altar, anoint a stone, they fence in the place
where God has appeared. The disciples of Jesus
believed in him and Mary anoints him in view of
his burial. Thus, and in many other ways, God reveals himself in a definite place and that place
changes when God touches it.

2. Further we must always remember that Scripture does not treat about Redemption as such, but
about Salvation as it is revealed in history. It is to
this that Scripture testifies. Revelation is present
and happens in the life and the movements of man.
God comes near, he thrusts himself upon man, he
wants to be intimate with man as he makes his
human pilgrimage through the centuries. He comes
down for that; he comes from outside, from on high.

He comes, indeed, from further away than we are able to think. He is more that we can suspect. He introduces himself in the dusty vestments of long, long years, and sometimes he must beg in order to be understood. But he is there.

History follows a certain course, God directs it, he guides it with a strong arm, in it he reveals himself to man. This action of his on the historical level is not restricted to one confrontation. God's coming does not happen once for all. We need not content ourselves for all times with one particular event. Every Revelation of God points again to another, announces another approach of God. When God comes, he promises to come again; when he makes himself known, he promises to make himself known further; he promises to fulfill what he promised the first time.

Every appearance of God therefore points beyond itself: it always goes on in a certain movement along a line which we can follow through all the centuries. The bearing points of that long line are the moments in which God has shown himself to man. He establishes this line and makes it clear to us that the history of this world rests in his hands.

When the people of Israel are being oppressed in Egypt and are only able to utter a suppressed sob, God in heaven hears this tearful prayer and remembers the covenant which he made with Abraham, Isaac and Jacob. He shows himself to Moses in the fantastic glow of the burning bush; once more he makes himself known as the God of Abraham, to reassert in this way the line which connects past and present.

When Moses is afraid, God comforts him with heavenly confidence: I am with you; you should come to adore me on this mountain.

And we know this: on that mountain the Lord again confirms the line which he has drawn; he makes himself known as the one who liberated the people of Israel from the captivity of Egypt; that is his title of honor, his glory from generation to generation. . . . His faithfulness lasts eternally; and his merciful grace never ceases.

When Jesus ascends into heaven and the apostles stand there, staring into heaven, and the thought comes to them that now the Lord has gone away from them, a messenger from heaven tells them not to stand there gazing, because Jesus shall return in the same way they have seen him going up.

Thus the line goes on throughout the centuries, to eternity. It is not only a line which runs through the centuries, not only a line of events on the temporal level. It is always God who makes himself known to man, who reveals himself to him and, in order to do so, takes the vulnerability of man as the measure of his actions.

Human roaming and human desire for peace beyond a far horizon is the situation God used to make himself known to man. The roaming existence

in this world, the feeble protection of a black tent
in the desert are the measure to which he adapts
himself. He wants to take part in his people's roaming through the desert and share their existence as
they seek a way through barren regions. He assists
them when they must fight to pass through a rough
and difficult country, longing for peace and the
fruits which they might one day pluck in a country
of their own.

In this way God has made himself known. His
saving grace travels along the road of human
roaming. That is why this road is more than merely
a road. It is more than a connection between two
points whose distance can be measured by earthly
measure. The road broadens into a way of salvation, it becomes a road along which grace is communicated.

Then the road takes paradisic features. Enemies
melt along that road like wax in the sun and heaven
drips mercy for the people along the road. The
earth quakes and the mountains of the gods are
envious at the thought that they shall not be chosen
as the goal to which this wondrous road leads. Upon
that road bread falls from heaven, mysteriously, a
continuous enigma, an enigma which shall remain
till they arrive in the land where they shall find rest.
We know why the bread was called "manna."
"Manna" is a hebrew word which expresses a question. It means "What is this?" and therefore the
Jews called this bread the what-is-this bread, until
it stopped falling on the other side of the Jordan.

That road is a special road, a road of salvation.
We can see that. The waters of the Red Sea recede,
the river Jordan divides its waters. The sea looks
and flees, Jordan turns back, the mountains skip like
rams and the hills like lambs. Everything trembles
at the presence of the Lord of Jacob, who turns the
rock into a pool of water, the flint into a flowing
well. God makes for himself a road, a wondrous
road. The wonders of paradise become a reality.
When the people become tired of roaming about,
and have arrived in the safety of a country of their
own, when victory is gained and they are satisfied,
when they sit in the shade of their own trees and
enjoy the fruits of their own land, then God again is
present in the peace they enjoy. Then he is intimate
with them as one is who after many roamings has
found peace in this world. Then he communicates
with them as one does who rests with his friends
or, better, who makes himself known as somebody
who invites others to live with him, who invites
people to be members of his household, to dwell
in his courts.

Then he is like a gentle Father, or like a good
king. People enjoy with him a deserved and well
earned rest. They live in splendor, almost in heavenly
bliss. . . .

One thing is clear: if God wants to dwell some-
where, he must build his house himself. Who among
mortals can handle the measure with which the
divine dimensions must be gauged? Who has power
to comprehend the length, the breadth, the height

and depth of God's love, which surpasses all understanding, if not God himself who chooses his archi-
tects, if not God himself who builds his house? Unless
the Lord builds the house, those who build it labor
in vain. Unless the Lord watches over the city, there
cannot be safety, the watchman stays awake in
vain. Therefore, when building the temple, people
must make it after a pattern which has been shown
to them: an earthly pattern is not sufficient.

In the house which God builds himself he can live
in splendor. There he reigns all powerful. There
he is enthroned, the angels sing about the fullness
of his holiness. The place where God dwells is holy.
Is it strange, then, that this place too should be
pictured in paradisic terms? Is it strange, that mar-
vels happen here, of which we can only dream as in
paradise? There angels keep watch: Cherubim,
just as at the gate of paradise. There flows an abundance of water, as can only be expected in paradise.
There one can be safe, because there is the unassail-
able protection of God himself. Therefore people
can answer those who provoke them, that the Lord
has established his holy mountain and that the people
at all times can find there a safe refuge. For with
him there is victory and strength. And his word and
his blessing, his strength and his grace proceed from
there, proceed from his holy abode.

These are the three aspects of God's historical
activity which we illustrated by means of some examples from the holy books. We have tried to under-

stand something about the images, and the meaning
that is hidden in them.

But perhaps we still should point out the over-
whelming character (as Scripture sees it) of this
historical revelation of God. This "overwhelmingness"
is its dominating feature. All pronouncements about
God and holy things are measured by this.

This revelation by means of historical events is
not, in some vague manner, just an indication of a
general belief in God, which man had "anyway." If
we want to speak about God and holy things as holy
Scripture speaks, we cannot look at it in that way.
Then we must confess that all speaking about God
must find its norm in the historical actions of God
toward man. Anything we can say about God is
derived from that. In speaking about paradise,
therefore, we must speak in accordance with Scripture. If we want to understand what Scripture
thinks about paradise, we must take our norms from
what is said in the first pages of Genesis and from
what is said elsewhere in Scripture about the historical actions of God.

We find a good example of this in the way the
ancients speak about the "how" and the "why" of
creation. The Israelites have at this time learned
to speak as inhabitants of the land, and they know
that in the beginning the Spirit of God moved over
the face of the dark waters. Then God separated
the waters and made the dry lands appear: the earth
is there.

See now how Scripture describes this. We find repeated here the rhythm of the history of grace: just as God once made a path for his people when he led them through the Red Sea, so also he made the dry land emerge when long ago he created the world (Is. 51). God's historical actions in favor of man are taken as the pattern for the description of those actions of God which we could call more general. Speaking thus in terms of historical grace is more than an accidental peculiarity of the holy books; it is essentially connected with them, and we are not able to understand those books, unless we take this into account.

3. The third point could be called a special illustration of what has just been said. Until now we have spoken about God who acts with man, who stands as security for a certain people, who helps this people and prepares them for his grace. But this is clear: these are a special people. Not a common people, but a chosen people, with whom God has made the holy Covenant, whom he has set apart, in whom he took a special interest. It is a people whom he has liberated from the house of slavery with a strong arm, and whom he has freely purchased for himself. In this way he has selected this special people as his own property.

He has willed that the way this people lived, dreamed and longed should be the way in which grace should be communicated.

Judging from this people we should see how good

the Lord is; how he approaches people and deals
with them; how it is when God wants to be intimate
with certain people.

God desired to share the fate of the sons of Abraham. He willed to reveal himself in the dark longing
of that great patriarch, who dreams about a posterity
during a night when the stars are shining. He revealed himself during Abraham's dizzying anticipa-
tion, when he let the sand of the seashore run
through his fingers: so numerous will his posterity be.
God has chosen this people and we have to submit
to this choice, which has also been decisive for us:
the promises have been made to Abraham and to
his seed.

From the epistle of Laetare Sunday we know
what is meant by this. St. Paul writes to the Gala-
tians that Scripture speaks here about Jesus; we
hear about this every fourth Sunday of Lent. Therefore the history of this people plays an important
part in the explanation of the holy books which have
ripened among this people. This people has designed these books for us and preserved them, in
order to let them speak at the time of fulfillment.
The people of Israel and the posterity of Abraham
were the keepers of the seal of God's promises. We
find them still, standing as faithful guardians, pondering at the entrance of our gothic cathedrals:
the house of God.

We spoke about God's sanctifying actions: how,
when he comes to us, the world acquires a new

splendor; how he communicates himself in the historical happenings of this world, and how he chose as the principal witness of all these actions the people of Israel; how he concerned himself with Abraham's seed (Is. 43, 10).

We could summarize this in a text from the letter to the Hebrews: that God has not been ashamed to be called their God, for he has prepared for them a city (Hebr. 11, 16).

Reading this, we know that we also must think about the vision of Jerusalem, the city in the mountains of Judah: the final goal of the long roaming of the people, a resting place after the arduous wandering in the desert, during forty years — the span of a man's life. But next to this glory, next to this sanctifying realization, we can find in holy Scripture another possibility.

Indeed, God's actions do change the world, but not always unto a blessing. Early in the Scripture story we see a significant illustration of this. We read there about Abraham and his nephew Lot. The land is not sufficient to sustain the flocks of both, and the shepherds quarrel among themselves. Then Abraham comes to an agreement with Lot, and Lot chooses the plain of the river Jordan. See, now, the description of this plain. There is an abundance of water; it looks like the garden of the Lord himself, it reminds us of the land of Egypt, where an ingenious system of canals irrigated the land. But see what the author mentions, as if in parenthesis: "This was before the Lord destroyed Sodom and Gomorrha" (Gen. 13, 10). The tension further increased when we note that Lot sets up his tents in that land, even though the people of Sodom were very bad and sinned against the Lord.

We know what happened (Gn. 19, 27). Early in the morning Abraham goes outside, looks in the direction of Sodom and Gomorrha and all the land of the valley, and sees the smoke of the land going up like the smoke of a furnace. And he understands that God has rained fire on the earth, in order to destroy those cities, because they sinned grievously against the Lord.

The horrible example of these cities will remain before us throughout holy Scripture, even in the New Testament.

The Psalms keep reminding us of God's anger; the enemies of God should fear this.

But the climax of the tragedy is the fall of The City itself: Jerusalem, the joy of all the earth, stands ablaze. The anger of the Lord was bound to flare up against the city and against Judah; the Kings kept sinning against the Lord, just as their fathers had done. It was unavoidable, and like a singeing blaze God's punishing breath passes over the land; nothing remains of the temple, the house of his glory, but smoking debris.

We must always keep this tragic possibility before our eyes, when reading and meditating Scripture.

God's action is not always paradisic; it can also change into its opposite, because it must be understood in human history. People must say "yes" to it. Men must acquiesce to his activities when he prepares himself a place. Speaking in the images of Scripture, people must erect an altar, anoint a stone. If not, his angry fire descends. Man must fulfill certain conditions, keep certain rules; otherwise he breaks the spell, and the harmony collapses.

We have seen the conditions which, we think, must be complied with in order to be able to speak about paradise as the holy Scriptures speak. This we know: paradise probably becomes something different from what we may have thought. It is not only the enclosed garden of Eden, which was planted in the beginning by God, and where there are trees: a tree of the knowledge of good and evil and also the desired tree of life. If we take these conditions into account, paradise becomes a quest of the holy enclosure which God has established. It becomes a meditation about an enclosed garden, which God had chosen as his property. Looking at it in this way, paradise also finds its place in the prospect of the revelation God made to Abraham and his seed.

2

THE MINISTERS
OF THE WORD

It is not sufficient to indicate the rules for thinking about these things. We must also pay attention to the way in which these things are described in holy Scripture.

We have already said that the holy books give witness about God's revelation, about the information he has given us about himself. They witness to the intimacy which he wants to have with us, and they relate how throughout history he has been seeking his people in order to be together with them.

Holy Scripture shows us the line which runs through history. It shows the line along which God has made himself known.

Now we can see how this line has been described by the ministers of the word, how it comes to life in the words of the prophets.

In order to draw a line, two points at least must be designated. And when we deal with history in time and the line has to be drawn through time, we must know the second point, before we can draw the line from the first.

This seems clear when we read holy Scripture. In the flames of the burning bush the Lord makes himself known as the God of Abraham, of Isaac and of Jacob. It is not difficult to understand that first the bush must burn without being consumed, before we can decide that there goes a line from Abraham in his tent who received the three angels and wanted to wash their feet to Moses in the desert, who had to take off his shoes. And it is equally clear that Abraham can only be called father of our faith if we are prepared to believe this.

This is not a matter of finding in Scripture short stories, interesting tales about old patriarchs and the revelations they may have received. The problem is in the first place, to find the function which they have in the great whole, to find the place they occupy on this line, the golden thread which runs through Scripture. Scripture is not simply a description; the authors, as it were, are always looking back. They always keep their eye on the road which has been travelled; they try to see back along this road from the point at which they have arrived.

One might therefore say that holy Scripture has been written backward. One first has to know something about the last point, the goal, before one can describe the preceding facts as having been directed toward it. One must have arrived someplace in order to be able to state that the road one has travelled had lead indeed to the point of arrival. One must in a certain way have been placed in possession of something.

The sons of Jacob must have conquered Jerusalem in order to be able to look back at the road they travelled toward it.

The author must have a certain intimacy, a certain familiarity with the Lord in order to be able to describe that this is the fulfillment of what was promised before and had been announced before. In this way, and only in this way, can we describe this line, notice the strong golden thread. Whoever writes in the holy books tries to let this line speak up, in order to express the things we can now read in it.

This means that the descriptions of the holy books are not just descriptions. The author is not interested in description. Above all, he is not interested in writing what the weather was like when Abraham started on his voyage and how many degrees the temperature was during the difficult march of the Israelites through the desert. The authors are not reporters. It is even a question whether we should expect this. Writing is, after all, never a bow to the obvious. Writing is something more than mere grasping of what lies within our reach. The authors of Scripture, too, were subjected to this rule. Writing is something more than looking at reality from all sides. Writing is penetration into reality by means of words. It is an attempt to puncture the epidermis of reality. It is an endeavor to put into words that which lies beneath the surface; it is like plowing by means of the word. Different layers of the earth are turned up; the pressure of the surface, it appears, had hidden the different layers from our view. Only the strength of the word could reveal them. Writing is a quest by means of the word, an effort to give something in words, to render something in words, to pass on something in words. Sometimes we have to wait to find whether it is possible to put something into words or not. Sometimes it is necessary to be quiet and hope that something will be worded, that something can speak to us. We remember the receding vision of the Lord on mount Horeb, where Elijah witnesses a strong wind which cracks the mountains and shatters the rocks, an earthquake which leaves nothing untouched, and fire which consumes everything. The Lord God speaks only in the gentle breeze which follows; proverbially, in this way he manifests himself to the zealous prophet. But the prophet had to make a long journey for it and to climb a high mountain. Only on the mountain did it become clear to him what all that had happened meant. This is what happens to many writers of the Scriptures. They must go and see, just like the prophet Elijah; then they can see further and they see more than before. They can see beyond the obvious; they can discern features in the landscape which are hidden to those who remain down on the plain. So they are able to penetrate deeper into the landscape by means of the words. Writing, they can map out the road which has been travelled; everything is spread out before their eyes.

This is what happens to the ministers of the word. The word never is merely a copy of reality. It is

never similar to reality. It **is** reality. That is, it is
reality by virtue of speech, by virtue of the word,
spoken reality. The line which we called the golden
thread, which runs through the Scriptures, exists in
Scripture only in speaking. That line is only visible
in the light of the word. The authors have un-
covered this line through their word and their
language. The golden thread glitters, because it is
described as glittering in the holy books. We can
ask ourselves what would have become of it if
nothing had been written about it. Maybe we would
then have a few loose stories, erratic fragments.
But, taking those into our hands, we would have
experienced something of the disappointment we
feel when looking at ruins: fragments and debris,
but the key to put them all together is not there.
Our quest would be in vain. But now that the line
is apparent, all the stories of Scripture find their
own place again. In this way they become so many
stopping places along the road toward the ever
growing intimacy the Lord wants to have with us.
It is like a line of revelation, a line which connects
the actions of God, a line which wants to show that
it is everywhere the same God, and wants to throw
light upon his faithfulness, that lasts from generation to generation. This line shows that it is the
same God who leads the Israelites away from Egypt
and who protects them from all the enemies around
the promised land. This is something that does not
arise in the heart of man. It comes from heaven, it
comes down to us. Our part in it is extremely small.
It is the revealing power of God, and what could our

part in that be? It is clear therefore that this line
cannot happen to just anybody. It requires a vocation, one must be set apart for it. God must occupy
himself with a person in a special way before this
person is able to look back upon the road which
has been travelled, before he is able to understand
the road which has been travelled and to point out
that this is the road on which God has been leading.
One must have stood on a barren hill and witnessed
an apparition of God; one must have received a very
intimate vision. Only then one can see the thoughts
of the Almighty. Only when God speaks to man
does a spirit enter into him, so that he can stand up
to behold, to learn the intentions of God. Holy
Scripture gives us many examples of the different
ways in which God sets somebody apart in order
to let him see what his intentions are. And one
must know what God's intention is, in order to be
able to indicate the line of which we speak. Sometimes one must sleep along the road as Jacob did,
and receive a dream. Or one must fight with a
heavenly being, as happened to Joshua. And at
other times God is near, in order to put his words
into the mouth of his prophet. Then the mouth of
the prophet adapts itself to the word of God which
has been placed into it. He acquires the divine accent
and is able to speak about his intentions. God
touches the man whom he calls. By this touch of
God man is changed. He receives the stature of a
heavenly being and acquires insight into God's intentions. In this way he is able to point out various
things and he is able to look back in the right way.

His human helplessness changes into divine strength. This touch of God does not only make him into a special witness of the road which has been travelled; there are even moments when the prophet is allowed to see further, when he is allowed to see the end towards which the voyage shall lead. Sometimes he is allowed to see what awaits the people; he is allowed to tell them about this and to foretell what the future shall be. When this is written down it is no longer a question of being allowed to look back, to write backward. In certain cases it is possible to write about that which still must happen. This can be prophetical writing, a looking back from what one knows must yet happen. We could call this a looking back from the future.

Once the sons of Jacob have arrived in Jerusalem, the road along which they arrived can be described as a road of grace. But if one has been set apart by God it is possible to know something about the heavenly Jerusalem that is yet to come. Then one can interpret the road on which one is travelling now by judging from the glorious future. The one can, with the author of the letter to the Hebrews, say that Abraham, Isaac and Jacob have received the promise that they would be allowed eventually to live in a city, the foundations of which were designed and built by God himself. It is clear that this stretches much further than the horizon within which we see the earthly Jerusalem. The prophet has received insight into the plans of God; he can tell us about them and indicate the line further than the moment at which they have actually arrived. In this way we realize that it is necessary to have received a special grace in order to speak in this way about those things. It is necessary to have received the vocation to be a prophet in order to be allowed to speak thus. And for those who take part in the history, who are going along with the chosen people, such a prophet is necessary to indicate the road, to show them that they are travelling on a road which God himself has made. They simply cannot do without such a man of God, such a minister of the word, who is able to reveal the unseen: the Lord does nothing without revealing his plans to the prophets, his servants.

3

THE LANGUAGE OF CANAAN

We have explained about the ministers of the word. Nevertheless, we feel that not everything has been said. These ministers speak a certain language; they do not always speak in the same manner, their words are not always the same.

Not all languages are the same. Every language reveals in its own way the wonderful reality which is hidden under the veil which hides all reality. It is useful, and more than useful, to pay attention to the language in which the magnificence of God's grace has been sung, to look at the language in which God's mysteries are celebrated. We know the name of this language. It is the language of Canaan. This means the language of the promised land, the language which the Israelites began to speak after they crossed the river Jordan. It is the language which has something of the odor of the sons of Jacob about it; the smell of a Palestinian field which the Lord has blessed adheres to it. It is the language of conquest, the language of the conquered land. With the land, the Israelites conquered the language as well; they learned to speak that language, while building houses and tilling the soil. The fruits

which they ate from their own fields, which they
plucked from their own orchards, they could name
only in this language. This sounds like a truism.
But we are perhaps not aware that this might have
an added meaning. One might perhaps say that
nothing special is happening here. Such things happen in many places of the world; it is quite common
that a certain people takes over the language of the
country where it has settled.

But this is the chosen people, the people with
whom God wanted to make a covenant in a special
way. A people who were able to conquer the country only because God had promised this to their
forefathers. The Israelites are allowed to take possession of it in virtue of God's promise. In this
light the expression "the language of conquest" gets
a special sound. It is not just a technical means
to express oneself which one happens to have at
hand. This language, too, had to be conquered,
just as the country was conquered. The people had
to master it, and to live with this language in the
country which God had given them. They needed
this language in order to say what this country
meant for the people of Israel.

We have already spoken about "writing backward": the characteristic way in which the holy
books were written. Only in this way can we understand what is meant. Now in the conquest of the
promised land God's promise to the patriarchs received its magnificent fulfillment. This conquest
makes real what God said to Abraham: Rise, walk

through the length and breadth of the land, for I
will give it to you. This is a proof of God's love,
which surpasses all understanding. It is such a
magnificent fulfillment that the Israelites could think
that now everything that God had promised them
is fulfilled.

Now we undersand why we should be interested
in the language of Canaan. The fulfillment finds its
language, can be interpreted, finds a sounding board.
This is important, because this becomes the language
in which the Israelites look back. In this language
they look back over the road they travelled towards
the promised land; in this language they see this
road as a road of grace. In this language they learn
to speak about God, who keeps his promise, who is
faithful, and who fulfilled everything he ever promised to the patriarchs. And — what is more important still — in this language God receives his name
and his titles of honor. This is the language in which
the Israelites must give answer to the question "Who
is God?" and in this language the melodious answers
will resound. They will proclaim, first, that God is
the one who chooses; secondly, that he loves his
people so much that he did not want to leave them
behind in the slavery of Egypt, that he liberated
them and led them away to the promised land.
Finally, they learn to say in this language that God
wants to deal with them in an intimate way, that
he has made a covenant with them which shall stand
forever.

This is why this language is so important, even in

our "enlightened" times. We cannot overlook it.

In this fulfillment God has communicated himself. In this fulfillment he not only kept a promise of old times, not only all that he had ever foretold. This fulfillment once more points onwards and awakens in us too a desire for the future. This fulfillment, this conquering of the promised land, is itself again the promise of a revelation of a still more intimate nature, of a still more intimate communication from the Lord. This fact, namely, that this first fulfillment finds its language, that the Israelites after this first realization are able to stammer and to thank God in a language of their own gives to this language an expressiveness which is superior to the casual utility which every language has. They are able for the first time, as God's people, to pronounce God's own names. They can communicate with this God in a way which is meaningful to themselves. They have a special pitch for speaking with him. Their mouths adapt to this language, and their hearts must always be in accord with this tongue. In this language they are able to discover the line which is to be found in God's gracious dealing with them.

In this language they formulated the line which runs through their history. God will always continue to work along this line, because he never comes to abolish something; he comes only to bring something to its fulfillment, even though he sometimes does this in a way that is unexpected for us. This means that we too, when speaking about this line,

must tune our language to the language of the sons
of Jacob, which they conquered at the same time
they conquered the holy land, and which they used
to proclaim God's deeds. In interpreting this line
we must take care that our language speaks in
accord with the holy Scriptures. If we want to acknowledge that these Scriptures play a part in the
long journey which revelation makes through the
centuries, we shall be bound to acknowledge that
this language and this way of expression play an
important part.

It is obvious that the Israelites did not spontane-
ously formulate their language. They did not con-
struct it themselves. They took it from others by
conquest, they captured it, as they took possession
of the promised land. This language had already
been used before. It had already served as a means
to convey thoughts about gods and heavenly things.
But the Israelites really learned to master this language, to make it subservient to their own religious
thought. Of course they took over many expressions
and, just like the peoples around them, they spoke
about clouds, thunder and lightning when describing
a theophany. This could hardly be otherwise. To
take only one example: just like so many other
peoples, the Israelites thought that God lived in the
far north. But when they spoke in this way, the
obvious meaning of the words used had to defer to
the Israelitic concept of God. So we find that they
sometimes write about Jerusalem (Mount Zion) as
the city in the north: Psalm 48 calls Mount Zion

the city in the far north and the city of the great
King. Yet, for the Israelites Jerusalem lay in the
south. But they are describing the divine abode,
and thus it happens that the Israelites betray their
indebtedness to a very old religious way of speaking. They take these old customs over into their
own historical process.

The poets of the Old Testament make use of some
such colorful expressions which arouse our curiosity.
They can afford the luxury of being barely understood. But they use them in order to sing about God,
who led the people of Israel out of Egypt and gave
them rest in the promised land. This historical
exodus is the marrow of their religious creed. This
language plays a part in revelation, in God's coming to us. God wants to speak to us in this way:
he made use of these words. This also is a mystery
for which we must be grateful. If we want to learn
to understand him correctly we shall have to travel
the road over which he went to reach these words.
This language stands at the end of a voyage which
lasted a lifetime.

In conclusion we may say that the language of
Canaan is the language in which people can speak
about God's actions in this world, in which they are
able to praise the realization of God's promises, and
sing about the country God has given them.

4

A LAND LIKE THE
GARDEN OF THE LORD

During the conquest the Israelites learn to speak about God. In the conquest their language takes its shape; therefore this way of speaking can become the norm for all speaking about God, as is done in the Scriptures. Here we have our linguistic laws. Speaking about God and praising his mighty name has its source in conquest. As time goes on new generations arise and they also teach their children to sing the old songs. They hand on what they themselves heard from their forefathers. And in all these old tales the praising narrative about God who liberated the people of Israel from Egypt and led them to the promised land is the principal theme.

When we investigate the holy books, and try to find an answer to the question who God is, one chief answer emerges: God is the one who loved his people who were in slavery in Egypt, and he liberated them in order to lead them to the land that he had previously promised to the patriarchs. This is the standard reply which the Israelite father annually gives when his son asks him about the

meaning of the festive night of the Passover. This
answer the Israelites set as a seal upon their hearts,
it was carved into their flesh. They carried it as a
sign upon their hands, as a reminder on their fore-
heads, in order always to be able to praise the
realization of God's promises: that God liberated
them with a strong arm from Egypt, the house of
slavery. Every praise of God, every creed, finds
its norm here.

Therefore one formula of this creed which is perhaps the oldest we have in holy Scripture is very
significant. It concerns itself with the offering of the
first fruits, as described in Deuteronomy 26. This
offering (of the first fruits) is not something that has
its source in the exclusive character of the religion
of Israel. We meet this practice among many peoples
and among many of them it is an annual ritual, as
it is in Israel. But this people will remember every
year that they were allowed to pluck the fruits
of a country that they received from the hands of
the Lord, a land which was given them after a long
and dusty voyage through the desert. The offering
of the first fruits is real gratitude for this grace,
a thanksgiving for the gracious fact that God after
a long voyage gave them this land, these fruits. As
this chapter lies now before us, it clearly shows
traces of what we have said before. This passage
also has been written backward and the road through
the desert is recognized as a road of grace because,
starting on this road, the people already had before them the prospect of the promised land. While

on their way through the desert they were already
able to think of the promised land with all its promises; therefore this road, which often is so dusty,
already shares in the glory of grace. The Israelites
are told that they will be able to make a choice
from the abundance of fruits which the country will
yield and that they will have to appear before the
Lord with the first fruits, in order to proclaim in
all earnest: "I declare this day to the Lord, that I
have come into the land which the Lord swore to
our fathers to give us" (Deut. 26, 3).

After that the sacred author enlarges somewhat on
this praise. He relates how God took to heart the
misfortunes of their fathers who were about to stray
like a sheep that is about to stray from the flock.
He proclaims how God heard their prayers when
they were bent down under the burden of slavery
in Egypt. Then he bursts forth in shouts of joy,
because God liberated his forefathers, and all the
words which are found in the holy books before
this chapter are summed up, in order to make it
quite clear: "The Lord brought us out of Egypt
with a mighty hand and an outstretched arm, with
great terror, with signs and wonders; and he brought
us into this place and gave us this land, a land
flowing with milk and honey. And behold now I
bring the first of the fruits of the ground which Thou,
O Lord, hast given me" (Deut. 26, 8-10).

We have previously remarked that this country is
called by the Israelites a land that flows with milk
and honey. We are inclined to say: this is impos-

sible. We have seen this nowhere in the world, and moreover it is astonishingly improbable, notwithstanding the many learned solutions which some tried years ago to give as explanations of this expression. These pointed out that a drastic change of climate could have occurred in the countries of the Middle East. But we, possibly, can find the solution in another direction. We are speaking about a country which was given to this people by the Lord. This makes it automatically something very special. This country is God's property; he has given it to Israel as its inheritance. It therefore has to be different from the countries which surround it. And how should one be able to speak otherwise about the wonderful country which God himself has given to a certain people, except by saying something very special about it?

Another solution which lies closer at hand, is possible. "To flow with milk and honey" is an expression of the language of Canaan; it occurs very often in the holy books. Before the Israelites came, the inhabitants venerated gods who according to their opinion had charge of fertility. Fertility could only be given from heaven, and even if man were able to irrigate the land, the gods had to assist him. The gods took care that the furrows, which man dug, flowed with oil and fat, and that the land flowed with milk and honey. The expression "flow with milk and honey" seems therefore to mean, that a land is intended where irrigation is possible, but where the gods must lend fertility to the human

labor. In this connection we could point out Gen.
13, 10, which speaks about an abundance of water,
as in Egypt, and all this is called "a garden of the
Lord," a country therefore like paradise. And into
this garden the people of Israel are now allowed to
enter.

1. The shade of the true vine.

The Israelites realized how they came into possession of the country. They were fully aware how
God had fulfilled his promise. They dedicated a
whole book to the memory of Joshua. They venerated his memory because God had effected the
conquest of the land through him. God fulfilled his
promise through him to the very end; therefore
the memory of Joshua is venerated. This lends a
certain enchantment to the first entrance of the
promised land.

Hesitatingly, they approach. Moses has to send
out spies: one man from every tribe as a representa-
tive of the tribe of his fathers. He sends them out
of the desert into the land. And the holy books
remind us that it was exactly the time of the first
ripe grapes (Num. 13, 20). This means it must have
been autumn when the representatives of the tribes
received this order to reconnoiter the land, because
grapes do not ripen before autumn. Further we
might note that this has also something to do with
the place where the Israelites first arrived. That
place bears the melodious name of "bunch of grapes"
(**Eshkol**): how would the Israelites have thought up
this name if it had not been the time of the first

grapes? But for us, who want to accept the old books as a foreshadowing of what is to come, it is possible to surmise already here something of the wonderful true vine, who will be announced to us afterward as the Good News. Therefore, not only grapes: grapes point the vine from which they are plucked. And they lose their strength when they are taken out of its shade. This is something of a fairy-tale; it can only have happened long ago.

And Joshua plays an important part. His real name was Hosea, a very common name. It means salvation; but even his name is not able to express the task placed on his shoulders. In view of this wonderful task, the reconnoitering of the promised land, Moses changes his name and calls him Joshua (Num. 13, 16), "he shall save," a name in which we can savor the power of the Lord, in which we feel his helping hand, in which he carries and protects his people. That name is a form of the word "save" and holy Scripture remarks about it just before the struggle between David and Goliath, "that all the earth may know that the Lord saves not with sword and spear; for the battle is the Lord's and he will give you into our hands" (I Sam. 17, 47).

This name is imposed upon Joshua because of the kind of task imposed upon him. The Greeks, in their blessed translation (the Septuagint), have noted that Joshua bears the same name as Jesus. The ful-filler of the old promise is called by the same name as he who in the New Covenant announces the first fruits of the final fulfillment. The old Fathers of

the Church have pondered upon this — and, we
can say, not without cause. We know that Joshua
was not accepted and that with Caleb he rent his
clothes when the Israelites did not want to listen
to their report: they preferred to listen rather to
those who did not bring them good news, who told
the people that the country which God was supposed
to have promised them could not possibly be reached
and that they simply were not able to conquer it.
Joshua rent his vestments, because his name is both
a symbol and a proclamation. He must have been
sad because his people dared not live according to
their holy history, a people who had no confidence in
God, and who through Moses had given him the name
Joshua, because it is the Lord who decides the battle.
This people does not dare to have confidence in the
faithfulness of God who will always march at their
head. They do not dare to follow God when he
sets out conquering, they do not dare to let themselves be led by him who has always given them
victory. Is not he the God who makes the hearts
of his enemies melt as snow in the sun? But now
we see it is the hearts of the Israelites that melt,
whose courage sinks. They do not dare to go on.
And Joshua is sad; he rends his vestments; was not
the secret of the conquest entrusted to him on the
threshold of the tent of revelation; from the midst
of the mysterious cloud? It would seem now
that he cannot carry out his mission. He was told
to be brave and courageous, because he had to
lead the children of Israel into the land that God
had sworn to give to their fathers. In these words

we hear the echo of the order for the holy war, the order for the conquest. It is clear that in this tradition all the attention is on Joshua, who plays such an important role in this conquest. It is therefore not strange that all this is solemnly repeated in the book of Joshua. In the first chapter we read a few times that God shall be with him, as he also had been with Moses, and he is enjoined again to be brave and courageous. This means that in this expedition he can trust in God's protection, that heaven will assist him, and that the stars will fight at his side. God marches at their head and who shall resist him? Joshua can begin the expedition to the promised land when there is nobody left of those who resisted his good news — those who did not want to see the bunch of grapes as a token of the vine, the glory of the promised land. They resisted the holy promise and we know how this was reckoned against them.

We can expect that they passed the frontier of the promised land with a certain solemnity. God tells Joshua that on the day they pass the river Jordan, he shall begin to make him great in the eyes of all Israel, so that they will know that God is with him as he was with Moses (Jos. 3, 7). And as Moses was allowed to pass through the sea in order to show that the horrors of Egypt now lay definitely behind them, so also Joshua was now allowed to cleave the waters of river Jordan in a solemn manner, because now the fulfillment begins, now the promises approach their fulfillment. It is a moving scene, this first contact of Joshua with the soil of the promised land. Before Jericho is taken, an interview with a heavenly being is granted to him, a warrior of the heavenly host. And Joshua falls down in adoration, takes off his shoes, because the place where he stands is holy (Jos. 5, 13-15). How could it be otherwise? He has now arrived in the holy land.

Then the manna stops falling. Questioning gives way to knowledge; the people now may eat of the fruits of the holy land. When all the conquests of Joshua have been described, the Book mentions that the Lord gave the whole country to his people. "And the Lord gave them rest on every side just as he had sworn to their fathers; not one of their enemies had withstood them, for the Lord had given all their enemies into their hands. Not one of all the good promises which the Lord had made to the house of Israel had failed; all came to pass!" (Jos. 21, 44-45). And when Joshua comes to the end of his miraculous strength, he calls together all the elders and heads, the judges and officers of Israel. And he tells them: "I am about to go the way of all the earth, and you know in your hearts and souls, all of you, that not one thing has failed of all the good things which the Lord your God promised concerning you; all have come to pass for you, not one of them has failed" (Jos. 23, 14). Not only must they remember their liberation from Egypt, but first and foremost the wonderful fulfillment of all the promises of God.

And this divine presence, this intimacy of the Lord with his chosen people, they try to perpetuate in a covenant. This presence of the fulfillment they try to stabilize in a solemn agreement. And according to the description of the last chapter of the book, Joshua again plays an important part during his very last days. He is allowed to be, as Moses once was, the mediator of the making of the Covenant in the promised land. God has made himself known by giving them the land. For the people of Israel he could be thought of only as one who is so good that out of sheer goodness he gave them a country; a country for which they did not labor, the cities of which they did not build, and yet they are allowed to dwell there; the vineyards and the orchards they have not planted and yet they eat their savory fruits (cf. Jos. 24, 13; Deut. 6-11). So good is God!

If we ask who he is, the answer can only be: he is the one who gave us all this. He cannot be thought of except in connection with this country, and his revelation cannot be thought of except in connection with the fragrance of the rich Palestinian fields. To serve him, is to serve him in this country. To serve him, is to keep up this country, to protect it and to till it. To leave him, to forsake him, means to place oneself outside the reach of the generous gesture with which he gave this land to his people. To forsake him, means to place oneself outside his protection. Then the angel lets his sword fall. When they leave him, they must leave this country. Living

there becames impossible for them, because it is
his property.

Thus this moving chapter (Jos. 24), sounds like
the responses in a litany of God's omnipotence: "We
will serve the Lord, for he is our God." Now we
can to some extent surmise what this might mean
in these circumstances. They will serve the Lord
and they will listen to his voice. "So Joshua made a
covenant with the people that day, and made statutes
and ordinances for them at Shechem, and Joshua
wrote these words in the book of God and he took
a great stone, and set it up there under the oak
in the sanctuary of the Lord. And Joshua said to
all the people: 'Behold this stone shall be a witness
against us'" (vv. 25-27). Here we can read how
the people of Israel have been thinking about the
possession of the holy land, what they thought about
the necessary conditions to be allowed to live in
the protecting shade of the Most High. We see
here what we consider the typical grace of a blessed
country, what according to their thought was necessary in order to be able to speak of a garden which
was planted by God himself.

These thoughts and these concepts formed their
religious feelings, and taught this people of that
country to speak about God. The laws are full of
these conditions: "If you walk in my statutes and
observe my commandments and do them, then I
will give you your rains in their season, and the land
shall yield its increase, and the trees of the field
shall yield their fruit. And your threshing shall last

to the time of the vintage, and the vintage shall last
to the time for sowing; and you shall eat your bread
to the full, and dwell in your land securely" (Lev.
26, 3-5). Wild animals will not prowl, there will be
peace on all sides, and enemies will not lie in wait
with drawn swords. In this paradisic climate the
Lord will look down upon his people, make them
fertile, and multiply them, and thus he will keep
his part of the promise; he will make his abode
among them and deal with them intimately. . . . "I
am your God." The actions of the people are the
condition, the human side of this wonderful covenant, in which God may be known and recognized.
One knows him in the fruits which he gives, in the
gentle dew over the land, in the breaking of the
bread one is allowed to eat. But when they do not
want to listen, when they despise his commandments,
then their eyes will lose their luster, they will no
longer see the splendor of the land, they will not
be able to live there anymore; their sowing is in
vain, and the enemies will take possession of their
property. God wanted this country to be the place
where he would deal with his people; the land
of promise rests on this encounter, and it can stand
only in virtue of this covenant.

If the sons of Israel for some reason do not keep
this Covenant, it breaks. The harvest does not yield
grain, the vineyard does not give its wine in season.
God destroys the vine and the fig tree, the country
is rent asunder and it becomes a prey for wild
animals, who devour it. Enemies prowl.

When a prophet has to speak in abstract visions about an impalpable grace, he knows nothing better than to write about the plower who is immediately followed by the mower, and about the winepress which is followed again by the sower. The mountains drip with new wine and all the hills melt. But in this way we already look beyond our own time, we are too hasty. . . .

In any case, as we have seen, the promised land and the divine grace which is given there, is pictured in the image of a few palpable fruits, in peace from enemies roundabout, in grapes and figs, in being allowed to live in one's house and not to be disturbed by wild animals. This is the background, against which all further development in their way of speaking must be seen. What we have from Joshua is not sufficient. After the fulfillment which came with him, the people continue, they go on writing history. The conquest of the country is intensified. We might say they are also able to conquer the country culturally. They now know how to speak about their possession in the proper way, they know what to speak about and what not, and they have taken over the customs which belong to this country. Then the Israelites want to have a king, just like other peoples about them, because they want to be like the others. And this longing becomes a refrain, which tells us the value of their development and progress: "We want to be like all the other nations" (1 Sam. 8).

But according to the Scriptures one cannot describe a king without referring to conquest; he is one who must play a decisive role in the fulfillment which has been promised by God. He gets a place in the long line which runs through history, and we must measure him according to this line.

2. A king who can carry the country.

The people get their king. The first is a giant of the tribe of Benjamin, a tribe which was not insignificant; he must seek to return the lost she asses of his father and we see what can happen to a man who meets a prophet on his path.

Saul is anointed by Samuel and becomes king of the people of Israel. He will be able to save the people from the hands of the uncircumcised Philistines. He is the first king. His election seems to be confirmed when he exposes and defeats the Ammonite Nahash (1 Sam. 11). The sinister name of this king means "serpent," and the serpent was more subtle than any other wild creature. We read about the proposal this serpent makes, about the shame he wants to bring upon the people. He wants everybody's right eye. Then the spirit of the Lord comes over the king: with his army he invades the camp of the Ammonites during the morning hours and he fights them until the heat of the day reaches its peak. Those who escape are dispersed in such a way that not even two of them remain together. But in spite of all this Saul is rejected; he refuses to carry out the divine order to the end. He refuses to carry out the divine order to "blot out the remembrance of Amalek from under heaven" (Exod. 17, 14).

He wants to reserve something of it for himself. And
God rejects the king, who could have been his
glorious servant. He leaves him alone in the battle.
The Israelites are beaten, Saul plunges himself on
his sword, and the mountains of Gilboa listen to the
moving dirge of the poet David. The dew shall no
longer come down over the mountains where the
heroes of Israel have fallen.

David bides his time in Hebron. Even before the
death of Saul, before the defeat of the people, it had
been evident to him that the spirit of the Lord
wished to rest upon him. Samuel takes a vial of oil
and goes to Bethlehem. There David is called from
watching the flocks. And Samuel anoints him in
the midst of his brothers, with the royal oil of
gladness. This David, who knows that he may be
a tool in the hand of the Lord, bides his time in
Hebron. There the elders of Israel come to him.
And before the face of the Lord they anoint him
king of Israel: human approval of the divine election. After he has been recognized as their king,
David at the head of his men attacks the city of the
Jebusites. It is written that David and all Israel
marched even against Jerusalem (cf. 2 Sam. 5, 6;
1 Chron. 11, 4). This shows what a glorious event
this march was for them. The taking of Jerusalem
is a feat which has received a significance which
must not be underrated in the traditions of the
ancients.

David was called "the fortunate one" because of
this feat; it is one of the reasons he became the

favored king. He takes a city in the mountains of
Judah, but this is more than just another successful
expedition. It can not be classified under the general
head "Further Conquests of King David." This
conquest was the apogee of all conquests. Taking
this difficult fortress, which could be defended by
cripples and blind people, is more than simply evidence of divine protection. It becomes the hallmark
which guarantees that God helps his people in conquering the country. It is like a divine seal, which
confirms the promise, binding together the different
ribbons and threads. And who shall break this seal?
God has attached it to his promises, who can resist
it? The Lord has founded Zion; it will not totter
in all eternity. All the promises ever made by God
are contracted as it were behind the protecting walls
of Jerusalem. Whatever held good for the promised land, now holds good in an enhanced measure
for this city. This historical conquest of David will
become the norm for all further conquests of the
holy land. The Israelites begin to realize this only
now that the country has come into their possession
entirely. They begin to understand that only after
the capture of this city can everything be considered
as complete. From within this city, from behind
these safe walls, they can look back and survey the
difficulties they overcame at the moment they
climbed the hills of Judah. Now a prospect lies
open before them and they will continue to dream.
From within Jerusalem they can see the fields of
Moab and perceive the road which leads from there
into the city, into the holy city. The city is holy,

even unto our days, because the Lord marched
at the head of the victorious armies of David. David's
power grew continuously, because the Lord was
with him. And after having entered the city under
this guidance, David realizes that the Lord has confirmed him as the king of Israel. Now he can realize
that the Lord has exalted his kingship for the sake
of Israel his people. Jerusalem, the chief conquest,
can now become the center of David's realm. It
can become the seat from which David governs.
It can be called the heart of the country. Ambas-
sadors of all countries come to king David; he ex-
tends his power on all sides, the peoples roundabout
become his satellites. He crowns himself with the
crown of the Ammonites, of Edom and Moab, the
hereditary enemies, of Aram and the Philistines;
even the cursed Amalek has to pass under his yoke
(cf. 2 Sam. 8). All of them bring gold and silver
to Jerusalem. The other tribes call Judah, the tribe
of David, happy. His hand is now on the neck of
his enemies. "Judah, your father's sons shall bow
down before you" (Gen. 49, 8). In the events of the
glorious years of David's kingship we hear the
faltering echo of old Israel.

The blessings of the old patriarch Jacob reach
into these times, they attain their fulfillment. This
glory of Israel the old Jacob, the true Israel, must
have visualized. These words are put into his mouth.
The father must speak the same language as the
son. And the son will not speak differently from his
father. Of course, these blessings were prepared

for the time of David. But in a deeper sense, the people wanted these things to have been said by the old Jacob. They emphasized the line which connects the patriarchs with the house of David in Jerusalem, a line which was protected and kept in existence by the God of their fathers. This is the chief thing. And then comes the moment when it is not important anymore, and this is the moment when one tries to interpret this line. At the beginning or at the end, it does not matter. One lays hold of a line, understands a continuity, one sees a road of grace at the end of which there is a city. The chief thing is to mark this road, to point out that it is a road of grace. We must disclose this road as the road along which God wanted to travel in order to communicate grace.

And then we hear again Jacob speaking about his son, about David the king: "Judah, is a lion's whelp . . . He stooped down, he couched as a lion, and as a lioness; who dares rouse him up? The scepter shall not depart from Judah, nor the ruler's staff from between his feet, until he comes to whom it belongs; and to him shall be the obedience of the peoples. Binding his foal to the vine, and his ass's colt to the choice vine, he washes his garments in wine and his vesture in the blood of grapes. His eyes shall be red with wine and his teeth white with milk" (Gen. 49, 9-12).

In order to describe the abundance of this kingship and to put into words the glory of the reign of David, one must pluck grapes from the vine.

The promised land yields only savory fruits. And
when we speak about the fruits of the promised
land, we see before us grapes that are being pressed.
This abundance, this royal splendor, this rest and
peace which go with it, leave nothing to be desired.
The people thank God for this realization. The
name of David becomes known in all countries and
with the help of the Lord the peoples begin to have
respect for him.

But David does not collect his men only in order
to conquer a capital. He does not collect the war-
riors of Israel only for the crowning event of the
conquest. He also goes with them to fetch the Ark,
to bring it with him to Jerusalem in solemn proces-
sion. The Ark of the Covenant must rest within the
city; he wants to prepare a resting place for the
sign of God's presence now that the people have
come to rest: the portable sign in which God could
reveal himself during the journey. We might say
that in this way the third stage of the conquest of
the promised land is reached. A first stage took
place when Joshua was allowed to enter the country
and the people praised the Lord for this realization
of his eternal promises. A second stage — in another
form — made the Israelites ask for a king and David
was anointed by the prophet; now, as God's special
servant, by conquering Jerusalem, he finishes the
third stage of the conquest which Joshua began
so gloriously. The wandering of Israel has definitely
come to an end. The road which began in Egypt,
when God remembered the covenant he had made

with Abraham, here finds its final goal; the city toward which Abraham unwittingly travelled can now receive a name, and it is called "Jerusalem."

But the conquest of the country may be interpreted in a still more intimate way as being the terminus of the road which God himself, veiled in his signs (viz. the Ark), has travelled. If we choose to see it in this way, the history of the people of Israel is the history of the holy tribal confederacy which was entered into at the foot of smoking Sinai. And the road of grace is the road along which the Ark travels — with all the people around it — from Sinai to Zion. A royal road! Seen in terms of the travelling Ark, God's grace takes the form of a special history, and we are able to interpret, in a special way, the history which God wants for his people. We can see the mystery of grace, when following the trail which the Ark has left behind it; a luminous trail in the darkness. And to this luminous sign a long reminiscence is attached. It is a reminiscence different from that of Joshua and the kingship, but just as real and just as faithfully kept in the holy Scriptures; another reminiscence, but equally formative of the foundation of God's holy dealing with his chosen people. In the books of the old Covenant these reminiscences join, they intertwine, and proclaim abundantly that God has visited his people.

The holy books mention that David, on the day that he transferred the Ark to Jerusalem, ordered Asaph and his colleagues to sing for the first time

the "Praise the Lord," a psalm which bespeaks the
mighty deeds of God (1 Chron. 16, 7); for the first
time a song which sings all gracious deeds. And
this in these circumstances! One feels that with the
transfer of the Ark a final goal has been reached;
and that is why for the first time the people are able
to narrate in one great movement all the prodigies
which God has wrought. They sing about the Lord,
who is good and whose mercy knows no end.

3.　The hallmark of the conquest.

With the conquest of Jerusalem the wanderings of
a people came to an end; at last they were, so to
say, at home. Now they knew in which direction
to look for the point where all their longings had
been satisfied. But the transfer of the Ark to
Jerusalem makes this city something more than the
capital of king David's realm. The city has become
the shrine where the Ark rests. Within her walls
the palladium of the people is kept in safety: because
of this she may better be called the holy city. Once
the Ark has been transferred to Jerusalem — a journey to be remembered by the people, in which they
rejoiced and which will become the model for all
the journeys which will be made to the holy city
afterwards — they are able to describe how the
Lord granted to David rest from all his surrounding
enemies, and a king can have his royal dream in
which God can speak to him.

David dreamed of a temple, a house he would
build for God, but God makes him understand that he

will build a house for David, and that the kingship of
that house shall be permanent for his posterity. The
son of David shall be king in eternity. This surpasses building a temple. This points to a Son of
David, who shall be greater than the temple, greater
than a building of wood and stones. God's choosing
faithfulness shall be more permanent than the stone
buildings of the holy city.

And then David prays his moving prayer: "There
is none like thee, and there is no God besides thee,
according to all that we have heard with our ears.
What other nation on earth is like thy people Israel,
whom God went to redeem to be his people, making
himself a name, and doing for them great and
terrible things, by driving out before his people a
nation and its gods. ... And now, O Lord God, con-
firm forever the word which thou hast spoken concerning thy servant and concerning his house, and do
as thou hast spoken" (Sam. 7, 21-23. 25). Let the
house of David be permanent.

And we know that the house which God promised to David was more permanent that the dream-
house of the king, who wanted to build a temple
for the Lord. Nevertheless, the temple is built. The
threshing floor of Ornan is to be the floor of the
temple: a place which, according to jewish tradition,
had been prepared by God from before the foundation of the world. Even the destroying angel of God
shrinks back from this place, has to stay his hand,
and this is the place where David is allowed to

plead for mercy for the city (1 Chron. 21, 14). This
is **the** place!

The son of David, Solomon, may build the temple
and realize his father's dreams. His name reminds
the Israelites of peace as well as of the idea of complete realization of God's promises. The word from
which his name is derived expresses the idea of making full, of being complete. Solomon after offering
the thousands of holocausts on the high place of
Gibeon (1 Kings 3, 9), has a dream and he prays not
for wealth and honor, but for an understanding mind
in order to discern the intentions of God regarding
his people. Perhaps this dream has something to do
with the plans he had, to build a house for the Lord;
a real temple, which could replace the shabby tent
of the desert. It was time to put away the attire
of the desert, and to build a house for God too, now
that everyone is able to live in a house and the
king has built a palace for himself. The relations
with the peoples in the surrounding areas are such
that Solomon is able to import men from foreign
countries in order to build the temple. The temple,
thus, will look somewhat like the temples in those
countries. After seven years of building the temple
of Jerusalem is ready. The Cherubim who stand in
the Holy of Holies stretch out their wings. They
cast their shadow before them, in order to protect
the Ark. Thus the Lord has found his resting place;
he takes possession of his house, and now has an
abode in the midst of his people. He lives, now,
in a temple.

But Solomon wonders, when the temple is dedicated, how it is possible that God allows himself to be captured in a place which has been designed by men. He ponders about this venture in which men have built this house of God. . . . From that moment God can live permanently with his people. Seen from this point of view, and under the golden shade of the Cherubim, we can surmise what an impression this must have made on the people — a people which has its God so near to itself.

And what held good for the promised land holds good in an intensified way for the temple of Jerusalem. We have already said that the idea of God's nearness runs throughout holy Scripture. Whenever we see something about God's presence, we must also read something about his desire to be with man. It is because he wants to accompany his people and wants to live with them, that he leads them along a paradisic road to a paradisic land. What a temple this must have been in which one was able easily to feel all this and adore God.

All blessings of the promised land are concentrated in the temple; all the blessings to be found in this world must be found in the Holy of Holies. There copious grace is distributed, there Seraphim glow with sheer devotion, and coals which can purify unclean lips are burning (Is. 6), to enable one to speak with the Lord. The summit of God's nearness is to be found there. All graces must be measured by this place, without fear of exceeding its measure.

It looks as if all longing has reached its goal, because
God lives tangibly among them. . . .

And round this temple live the inhabitants of
Jerusalem. They speak about the temple in their
own language. They speak in a religious language
about the God who lives there that has already been
spoken for centuries in the city. They speak about
the Most High God, who was served there centuries
ago by Melchisedek and who could be called the
Creator of heaven and earth. But they speak about
him in terms which suppose the glorious conquest
by the God of Israel. The measure remains the historical fact, the historical event which we can study
and classify. Prophets explain it to us and ministers
of the word announce it to us: Yahweh, the God of
Israel, after a long journey through the desert, has
taken possession of a temple, his house in Jerusalem.
From this great feat one can look back. One even
must look back from there, when there is question
about the very first things, the things which have
happened previously. Then God's dealing with his
people becomes the norm for speaking about whatever he did. The gracious deed of the conquest of
the holy land and of Jerusalem, the erecting of the
temple is a first datum, from which all other things
must be derived and judged. Every ascent to God
must be measured according to this. This going
up to the temple and this being allowed to be there
with the Lord, will furnish us with the words to use
when we want to speak about any other form of
being with God. In this way God revealed himself

in the beginning, in this way he told us about it from the summit of revelation, the temple. When Solomon has dedicated the temple he prays to the Lord and thanks him for his benevolence. He and his people are allowed to know God very intimately in his temple. Before all Israel he lifts up his hands to heaven and prays a prayer in which all the ideas appear which we have met already in the story of the brave Joshua. He prays for rain and fertility for the land. It might be possible that heaven should remain closed and no rains fall if the people have sinned against the Lord (1 Kings 8, 22); but if then they come to praise the Lord in the temple and there adore his name, he will listen from heaven and forgive the sins of his servant the king, and of Israel his people. He will again show them the road they must walk and give them rain on the land which he gave as an inheritance to his people. The idea of the promised land, and of the divine blessing which is poured out over it, is intensified in the temple, because even without any connection with the temple, we find these things in Scripture.

That is why, too, the shadow of misfortune hangs over this temple, should the Israelites find themselves unable to preserve God's gifts (1 Kings 8, 35). "If you turn aside from following me, you and your children, and do not keep my commandments and my statutes which I have set before you, but go and serve other gods and worship them, then I will cut off Israel from the land which I have given them; and the house which I have consecrated for

my name, I will cast out of my sight; and Israel will
become a proverb and a byword among all the
peoples. And this house will become a heap of
ruins; every one passing by it will be astonished and
will hiss" (1 Kings 9, 6-8). And if they ask why
this has happened to this people and this temple,
it shall be answered (and we notice the historical
argument): "Because they forsook the Lord their
God who brought their fathers out of the land of
Egypt, and laid hold of other gods." The Israelites
knew God and served him, because they knew he
had been good to them throughout their history
in the desert sands.

But the temple also stands in a poetical perspective. The touching language of the poets brushes
its walls in order to describe the wonderful deeds
of God that take place within. The poets must
describe how the glory of God filled the whole
temple; how the temple was different from other
buildings, and of what nature the temple should be
in order to bear this burden.

To express it in terms of our explanation: the
temple gets paradisic features. There is an abundance of water, and (this we know) which can only
be in a garden of the gods. Living waters spring
forth from the temple. There is a psalm (Ps. 46)
which sings about Jerusalem and the temple as a
divine fortress. Within that enclosure one is safe
in the divine protection. God is so near there that
nothing can ever happen to us. The flood of streams
which spring up there gladdens the whole city.

Because God is within it, the city and the temple will never totter in eternity, even if the kingdoms totter and the nations conspire. How could it be otherwise than that the enemies of the people stand in astonishment before this city, which is borne on lofty divine streams?

It cannot be otherwise: this foundation, his conquest and his people are dear to God. He loves Zion better than all the cities of Jacob. This world will take pride in being named after this city. All things that were said about divine palaces in the old language of the conquered country can now be said about the temple.

4. The city on the mount.

Can it be strange that the people of Israel in the days of King Solomon knew that what was happening was a fulfillment? A temple is built, God rests with his people, and the kingdom of David stands in all glory among the kingdoms of the earth. When they sing about this, its frontiers reach to the end of the earth. Consequently the frontiers are safe, there is nothing to be feared.

Judah and Israel were more numerous than the sands of the seashore; the blessing of Abraham's dream approaches its fulfillment; the Israelites ate and drank in abundance and they rejoiced, because Solomon reigned over all the kingdoms from the Euphrates River down to the land of the Philistines and the frontiers of Egypt. They paid tribute to Solomon and they were his subjects as long as

he lived. And because he ruled the whole territory
this side of the River from Tifsah to Gaza, with all
its kings, he had peace on all sides and the people
of Judah and of Israel, from Dan to Beer-sheba,
sat safely under their vine and their fig tree as long
as Solomon lived (1 Kings 4, 24-25). They can be
admonished to take care that this joy shall last.

They are admonished to keep all the commandments of the Lord, to preserve them and to study
them. Then they will be able to remain in possession of this beautiful land and leave it as an inheritance to their offspring. It looks as if nothing more
could be desired. All must look up to Israel, if they
want to know something about this wonderful goodness of the Lord. In all this meditating about the
promises Jerusalem takes an important place. All
thoughts about the divine fulfillment converge there.
Historically speaking, Jerusalem was in biblical tradition the last city that was conquered. It was
the last conquest, the most important one, the chief
source of David's glory which confirmed that the
country as a whole had fallen to the people. It was
a conquest which marked a definitive end. Reli-
giously speaking, Jerusalem is the holy city, which
is safe because the Ark and the temple are protected there. Jerusalem is the protection of the
divine throne. God wants to dwell there, therefore
the paradisic waters which flow in Jerusalem rejoice,
even though it has appeared necessary to take measures to provide the city with water.

For when God touches the earth, there is abundance, grace is nearly tangible. Jerusalem is the city on the horizon of the mountain tops of Judah; how wonderful is the city of their God. Beautiful stands the holy mountain, the proud peak in the north: God lives there; as we have heard, so we have seen in the city of the Lord of hosts, in the city of God, which God establishes forever.

Is it therefore strange that because of such a glorious fulfillment which the people of Israel experienced in the time of the kings a Jerusalem-mystique develops? The reigns of David and Solomon (and of many other kings besides) were the cause of it. The city is able to withstand its enemies; it stands, when all other cities totter. This is because it is carried by God and knows itself to be carried by him. Everything is simply taken for granted, when men speak about this city. It cannot be otherwise, because God has chosen this city to dwell in, has made it the fulfillment of all expectations of Israel. The ease with which we read the beginning of the seventh chapter of Isaiah, is significant. This is perhaps because the initial verses of the chapter explain intimately what it means: God with us, he who is able to let light shine forth even in the darkness.

The text says: "In the days of king Ahaz the son of Joatham, son of Uzziah, king of Judah, Rezin, the king of Syria and Pekah, the son of Remalia the king of Israel came up to Jerusalem to wage war against it." And in befitting pride, as if it could not be otherwise, they write: "They could not conquer it."

Because the fire of the Lord burns on mount Zion and in Jerusalem is found the fire for his sacrifices. This is how the people see the divine protection in the city. Jerusalem cannot totter; so they start pondering over this royal preference and Jerusalem becomes a wonder city on the far horizon. "Gird yourselves and be dismayed; take counsel together, but it will come to nought; because God is with us." The people ponder and the prophets formulate their words; they know about the people who stood at the foot of this Sinai in order to be stamped into a holy people, a kingdom of priests. This would play a part in the economy of grace of the centuries. One would have to look at the chosen people to know God. This was probably the reason it was chosen: to lead others to the house of the Lord, to make a road which leads to the special intimacy which God wanted with us. Now that the temple of God stands in splendor on the mountains of Judah, the prophets can begin to write about the last things. We, who are wont to understand the last things as the very last things of this world, are inclined to think that these are predictions which can only come to pass when the last day will be visibly near. We know too well that the hills of Judah could not lift themselves above the tops of other mountains, and nowhere is it written that all peoples have decided to proceed to Zion. But when we read the second chapter of Isaiah we see that he does not speak there about the end of time in our (let us say) traditional meaning of the word. The prophet Isaiah is not the only one who has spoken, in his vision about Judah and Jerusalem, thoughts inspired by God about the destiny of the holy city (Mich. 4).

The text says: "In the latter days." In my opinion we should not think here of the very end of this world, of something that accompanies "the last things." The expression "in the latter days" can be meant to express a certain fulfillment which is not necessarily the very last. It is the prophetical way of speaking to indicate the fulfillment which the seeing eye of the prophet could discern. Therefore the meaning of this expression can vary. We think that for a prophet like Isaiah — as far as we know him from other utterances, especially in the beginning of chapter seven — that it was difficult for him to look much further than the glory of the Jerusalem of his time. Also here the expression "in the latter days" means the present glory of Jerusalem, which the prophet feels he witnesses. Seeing Jerusalem in this way (and we can suppose that Isaiah represents the thought of many of his people) the mountain of the Lord or the temple of the Lord can be considered as being higher than the peaks of the mountains. All the nations flow to it and many peoples come and say: "Come let us go up to the mountain of the Lord, to the house of the God of Jacob; that he may teach us his ways and that we may walk in his paths. For out of Zion shall go forth the law and the word of the Lord from Jerusalem" (Is. 2, 2-3).

We see in this vision that Israel knows its function of being a mediator, and that it is aware of being a kingdom of priests, unto which they were called at the foot of Sinai. All people flow to it in order to receive grace through the mediation of the Israelite Law. They have to go to the holy city, because there, in the temple of the Lord, dwells the Lord. And the house of the God of Jacob stands far above all the mountains, visible to all, a city on the mountain which cannot be hidden. It looks like the dream of all times. They shall beat their swords into plowshares and their spears into pruning hooks. Every one then shall be able to have a share in that wonderful blessing of the promised land, which, as we see from the text, and also read in Micah, was a thought very dear to them, of which their hearts were very full. Everybody will be able to sit in peace under his vine and his fig tree. Nobody will terrify them. Indeed, so the Lord of hosts has spoken. "The Lord of hosts": this is the name they gave to God when speaking about the Ark and about the transfer of the Ark to the temple. This is now the name by which God, as the Most High, is known.

The texts which are inspired by this vision of the city remain in use even in our days; we still use them for our processions into the church, when we go up toward the altar. Among prophets this is called a vision and we like to describe it as poetical imagination. But the history of Israel has also expressed itself in this way. The authors of the history of the people knew that their city was carried by the Lord. They put this into words whenever they were saved in a special way. They always see the blessing hand

of the Lord, when the city is saved in a wonderful
way, however this may have happened. They pray
to the Lord in order to be saved, so "that all the
kingdoms of the earth may know that thou, O Lord,
art God alone" (2 Kings 19, 19). The important
thing is not that they shall be saved. We should
remember, that their God in those days could not
be thought of separately from this city, that his
name is the "Lord of Hosts," and that he has that
name because he led his people out of Egypt. He
has that name because of the exodus, because he
led this people into this town and not into another.
It is not just being saved they are concerned with in
the first place. They pray for permanence of his
grace, which consists in peace for Jerusalem. This
confidence with which they trust in the Lord is
evident in 2 Kings 19, 32: "The king of Assyria shall
not come into this city or shoot an arrow there or
come to it with a shield, or cast a siege mound
against it. . . ." The sign of this for the people will
be (we are used to it already) the blessings of the
promised land, the regular harvests and the fertile
rain: "This year you shall eat what grows of itself,
and in the second year what springs of the same.
Then in the third year (important events always
happen in a third period) will you sow and reap
and plant vineyards and eat of their fruits" (2 Kings
19, 29).

Forever shall be that vineyard, that vine to which
the king binds his foal, forever that wine, which
shall flow in abundance. It is shadow and fore-

shadowing of what must come, sign of all that is announced.   And   once   the   city   has   been   liberated,
they will again repeat the refrain of the psalm that
the Lord dwells in an impregnable fortress.

5

LOOKING BACK

1.   Darkness over the earth.

We should remember how Jerusalem is described. This is important, because from this city one should look back on the road that has been travelled. From it one must interpret the time which precedes the conquest. When in the prophetic vision the city glows on the top of the mountains, then the splendor of this blazing fire is strong enough to illuminate all the roads that lead to it. Then it is possible that the dark roads which have led to Jerusalem become transparent: one who stands on the heights of Jerusalem can see through them. It is evident that the way the people look at this city and describe it has its influence on the way they look at the road which leads to it. When one considers Jerusalem as the final victory, then one must describe the road to Jerusalem as an expedition of conquest. Only the end of an expedition can be a conquest. If one describes the city as guardian of the Ark of the Covenant, then the road which leads to the holy of holies must be described as a pilgrimage, in which the Ark is carried along.

But in all this we should not forget that we have

here a march of the people of God, and that there
is a point where they will finally find rest after
their long trek. They are a holy people, which God
has set apart for himself, to be his own property.
This people is allowed to have a wonderful relation
with God the Lord: the Covenant. He is the guaran-
tee for his people. He marches at their head; in
everything they are carried by him.

He makes himself known through his gracious
dealings with this people. He reveals himself in the
human history of Israel. When the people of Israel
march toward Jerusalem, we know they travel a
road which is being made for them by God. To be
fit for this function this road has to be of a heavenly
nature. If the city should be able to carry the
Ark and the house of God, it must flow over with
paradisic abundance. This is more than merely
representing the vine's tendrils on the walls of the
temple. This is a city and a country and a temple
to which the people have journeyed, because God
carried them along the road, like a father who
carries his child in his arm, or like the spreading
wings of the eagle which bears its young on its
pinions. Because Jerusalem stands at the end, being
blessed in a special way by God, and glowing with
heavenly splendor, one can, once arrived in Jerusalem, throw light upon the road that leads there.
Both aspects which are found in Jerusalem, of course,
play a part. Jerusalem, as the summit of the holy
land in the description of the conquest, ends the
road of grace which looks into the promised land;

Jerusalem, as the city which preserves the temple, where God has accepted a special house, ends the road which leads into it, which brings one inside the temple. Of greater importance are the "latter days" of which the prophets have spoken. Here is an end that represents a certain fulfillment. The road leading — to this fulfillment needs only to await this consummation.

When Miriam, the prophetess, takes her timbrel and repeats the mighty refrain which all the women sing after her when they dance, Israel shouts because of the miraculous redemption God has bestowed upon them by cleaving the waters of the Red Sea and preparing for his people a wondrous passage, an escape from bondage. Perhaps what they mean is the very fulfillment of that very moment. But once the people crossed the Red Sea dry-shod, holy Scripture already points to the road which begins (Ex. 15). The testimony of the Scriptures already mentions in that very moment what they have to expect, where the road will lead them, how this wondrous passage along which they have escaped becomes for them a road of saving grace that leads them to Jerusalem. They sing of this divine goodness, with which the people are being led by God, after having just now been saved. Then we read that he has saved his people from slavery in order to conduct them to his holy abode, and everybody knows what that means.

Trembling seizes the people; they hear what God has done. Pangs seize the inhabitants of Philistia, though in the future they will still harry the people of Israel. The chiefs of Edom are dismayed, as are the kings of Moab; all the inhabitants of Canaan melt away.

The way in which is described how good the Lord is to his people, how he deals with them, how he cherishes them and leads them, is significant for the way Scripture speaks about the holy land: "Thou," they pray, "wilt bring them in and plant them on thy own mountain, the place, O Lord, which Thou has made for thy abode, the sanctuary, O Lord, which thine hands have established" (Exod. 15, 17). We know this is a description of Jerusalem and of the temple which was founded there. There is a road which leads from the temple backward toward the sands of the Red Sea. The historical road is called "royal"; it is a heavenly road.

Balaam on his ass is called upon by Balak, son of Zippor, king of Moab, to curse the people of Israel on their way toward the promised land (Num. 22-24). Balaam is forced to admit that no incantation against Jacob is of any avail, nor any divination against Israel. He has to prophecy that this is a people on its way to a glorious future. He has to say that this is a people set apart by God; a people whose numbers cannot be counted; which is about to realize a far away future. And when the prophet Balaam lifts up his eyes and sees Israel with whom God has made a covenant encamping tribe by tribe, then before his eyes looms the vision of the holy land which God has promised to Israel. He sees the fairness of Jacob's tents and the glory of the encampments of Israel. Like valleys they stretch afar, like gardens beside a river, like aloes that the Lord has planted, like cedar trees beside the waters. Water flows from his buckets and his seeds shall be in many waters. The people which Balaam thus sees encamping is on its way to a paradise, is being led by God himself. Who will be able to withstand them? Certainly not the king of Moab.

Again, we might remark that the text, as it stands before us, probably originated in the land of Canaan and the words probably were put into Balaam's mouth by the men of Israel, as the Lord puts his words in the mouth of his prophets. But after all, this is not what occupies us here in the first place. The first question is, What does Scripture testify? Regardless of whether it originated in Canaan or not; the final text taken in this context shows the road which the people of Israel travelled in the desert, and interprets it as a road which leads to the promised land. The history of the people of Israel is shown us here as a holy history and we know that prophets are needed to give such testimony. It seems to me that only after this, in its proper place, does it become important to know the precise moment when some text was written.

Up to now we have not left Jerusalem; there we have tried to understand the testimony of the Scriptures. From there we have with the Israelites looked back over the road along which, under God's leadership, they arrived within the walls of the city,

within the temple of that city. In that temple we
have learned to sing God's praise. There we have
tuned our ears to his unmeasurable graces. We have
learned there how the Israelites learned to speak
about their country, their city and their temple.
We have heard there which images have, one after
the other, played an important part in this description. It has become a concrete thing for us. If we
say that God has prepared a place for his people, we
speak about the promised land and about Jerusalem.
When we speak about the road which God has
made for his people, we speak about the dusty road
along which the people travelled during forty years
through the desert. A dusty road, but royal, a road
which turned out to be a road of merciful salvation.
The holy place which God founds whenever he acts
in the world is called in biblical testimony the promised land, the physical, historically tangible land of
Canaan.

We know that God always fills with grace the
places which he founds. Perhaps we can now indicate what this means in the wording of biblical
testimony. It means that in that country there are
fruit trees, and we now know about the abundance
of wine, and how grapes are the sign of that wonderful abundance. We understand how a bunch of
grapes so heavy it needed two men to carry it describes the graces of the promised land. How God
creates a place, surely — but also how he planted
his graces there. Now we understand the prophet,
who sings about his friends, who can speak about

a love affair which he had with his Beloved: "My beloved had a vineyard on a very fertile hill. He digged it and cleared it of stones and planted it with choice vines; he built a watchtower in the midst of it, and hewed out a wine vat in it; and he looked for it to yield grapes, but it yielded wild grapes" (Is. 5, 1-3). Then we ask ourselves with the vintager what more could have been done than he had done, and we wonder with him about the sullen ingratitude that has been his reward. The decision, quite understandably, by the owner is destruction. He will no longer care for his vineyard. Briars and thorns shall grow up in it and its hedge will be removed. No rain will fall upon it, the clouds will pass over it without having mercy. Perhaps the story is clear to us. But Isaiah makes it still clearer. He says: "The vineyard of the Lord of hosts is the house of Israel (it is the name of God which goes with the Ark, in Jerusalem!) and the men of Judah are his pleasant planting; and he looked for justice but behold bloodshed; for righteousness, but behold: a cry" (Is. 5, 7).

The metaphors mix, but the main line is easy to see. We wonder about this prophet, who left us a vision about the end of time, about a grand fulfillment, about a closing point which illuminates everything with its splendor. This time he reckons with tragic possibilities, but nevertheless he keeps speaking about vine and grape . . . After all, though, we know their way of speaking. And we know how God directs history. He leads a people toward the

blessed garden within the enclosure of his vineyard.
He lets them rest in the shade of vine and fig tree,
but the same idea can be just as well expressed in
terms of transplanting choice vines.

The people of God is transferred, like a vine, in
order to be planted on the holy mountain of the
Lord, it is led from Egypt under the mighty protecting arm of the Lord and may then rest in the
land of promise. The saving action of God is sym-
bolized in the metaphors of the fertile land, and the
real history is worded in such terms in order to teach
us about things divine. God sets apart, in an actual
history, and this seems a mystery of grace, that
which can never be sufficiently stressed.

We have looked back from Jerusalem. It is possible to reach back so far that one touches the darkness of Egypt and hears there the moaning prayers
of the slaves. It is even possible to remember the
covenant which the Lord made with the patriarchs
and dream of the old Abraham in the starlit night,
where all the stars are called by the name of one of
his sons, or to sit with him at the seashore and see
how he lets the innumerable grains of sand glide
through his shrivelled hand. If we try to make our
gaze reach further, the darkness becomes too intense,
we cannot discern anything further.

We know there must be something beyond this,
because Abraham did not fall from the clouds. Other
men before him walked their road through the dust
of the ages, but they have become invisible for us,

receding inaccessibly far into oblivion. Some of them have left behind faint traces, fragments and ornaments of a beautiful past. We would like to know how God occupied himself with the very first human beings. We would like to know all that has happened to them and if much of today's misery has to be ascribed in principle to them.

We want to know the very beginning of things, to write an "In the beginning," the source, the principle from which everything else could be derived. We want to tell about this, to pass it to others, so as to keep it safe for those who will come after us, but we know, also, that the beginning of anything necessarily escapes us. The beginning we can never approach nor pass. We can never observe the passing of this limit. Mortals can never see the passing of a threshold, of a boundary river. To receive this gift, Jacob has to fight an exhausting struggle with a heavenly being, and after this he shall be a lifelong cripple. One has to be called for this, to be a partner of the saints, to stand amidst the prophets, in a place set apart by God for this purpose. If not, the beginning escapes us, it retreats whenever we think we have grasped it. Then we notice that we have a ripe fruit in our hands, not however a sprouting seed.

When we think we have caught something in the moment of transition, then the decisive transition has already been effected, because only after that we say that a transition has taken place. We can speak only about a beginning looking back from its fulfillment. Abraham, the father of those who want

to believe, can only be understood by those who
are children of faith. This holds good in any event.

When in our environment something starts sprouting, we do not discern this, because in order to see
it as a beginning we should be able to see its evolution in the future. And once the new thing has
grown up and we turn about to search back for its
first germ and its beginning we can never discern
those first phases. And still we would like to know
something about the beginning. We try to grasp
it, to lay hold of it. We reach out for it from the
situation in which we find ourselves and it looks to
us as we have laid hold of it.

We fix a beginning by judging from the final
situation in which we find ourselves. We could
compare this with the different ways of saving grace
about which we have spoken. In both cases, in the
song of Moses which was chanted by Miriam the
prophetess, as well as in the visions of Balaam, the
intention is to make clear that the Israelites are a
people under way toward a special blessing of God.
But in the first case the people is under way toward
the holy mountain: it may find a place in the
heredity of the Lord, and it may live in the sanctuary
that he has founded. In the other case it is announced that a delectable land of a paradisic nature
awaits the people. It depends only what stand one
takes, in order to interpret it one way or the other.
In fact we have here two different visions in holy
Scripture. But to this one can hardly object.
Both, in their divergence, keep up the wondrous line

which has been drawn by God and is cherished by
the people of Israel. A line of saving grace, which
after all can only be measured by a heavenly standard,
and therefore needs to be expressed in more than
one way in order to be understood by us mortals.
Should we wonder if one is always inclined to look
further back to try to discern the very beginning of
God's actions?

We know that this belongs to those things which,
in this world, are impossible. We try at our own
risk. It simply escapes us. We must fix a beginning
by judging from a final point. Judging from a
reached fulfillment we must fix a beginning which
shall serve as an explaining principle. The starting
point will be of the same nature as the fulfillment.
We simply have no other way of putting it. It is
the only way in which we may attain it. We know
how the people of Israel were able to discover God
in the experience of their own history. How they
were enabled to name God with names that form
their history. How they must name God with a
name from which their history becomes apparent
for us. It is the God who loved his people so much
that he was prepared to save them from the slavery
of dark Egypt. His name spells out the holy history
for us. Slowly we find out that the God who is
engaged in leading a people to a land of promise,
cannot be exhaustively known by the names in which
he has revealed himself. We can learn to know him
more and more intimately, and experience that there
simply is no other one like him, and that he also

occupies himself with other nations, that he holds
the history of the people of Israel in his mighty hand
as well as the destiny of the world. We have seen
this. But we also know the **why** of these provisionary
names. We know that the name under which he
was known to this people, was really his name.
Under this name he introduced himself provisionally.
If we want to know him further, we have to call
upon him by this name. We cannot avoid this. We
have to take this name on our lips, because under
this name he made himself known to those he had
chosen. He gave them a mediating function exactly
with this in view.

All speech about him must draw its measure from
these names. All that can be said about him depends upon and stands in the light of this historical
revelation. The history of mankind is integrated in
the name under which he is adored.

2. Back to paradise.

The holy Books speak about the first man. They
speak about that which has happened "In the beginning." We meet this as soon as we open the holy
Book. Be this as it may, we must realize that the
God of the first pages of the Book of Creation is the
same God as the One who made himself known in
the history of the chosen people. We opened the
book in the darkness of the Easter vigil, by the
glimmer of the Easter candle. Otherwise we simply
could not have read it. We should always remember
that Scripture has been written backwards. We

should realize that God is called by a name which he acquired while historically leading the people of Israel from Egypt. This people, which became acquainted with him in this way, may now start writing about him: how in the beginning he occupied himself with the world and with man.

They managed to reach these first things along the line which they were able to discover, along the road which once they travelled to reach Jerusalem. From this point they kept gazing back into the darkness of the centuries which had preceded. The illuminating cloud of God's presence, of his intimacy, showed them the way on this path of inquiry. Only in the light of this divine presence were they able to penetrate into the times and the days which normally escape our view. We cannot know anything about this, unless we are assisted by some such a bright light. We cannot discover the first man unless we follow the road which was travelled by the illuminating cloud. Only along this road are we able to find out how God dealt with the first man. Aside from this road nothing is to be found. If we depart from this road on which the cloud of God's presence guides us, we lose sight of the beginning. We go astray. We cannot but walk in that light, and thus describe the first things in accordance with Scripture, in accordance with what is written there. Only in this way can we understand how God worked in the beginning.

In order to speak about these things, we must take the correct standpoint, a standpoint from which we are able to look back far enough. We must choose a point high enough to look back so far that we can speak about "in the beginning." It seems to us that this is the way to speak about paradise. The road has reached the very beginning. God's first dealing with man must take place in the same manner in which he dealt with his chosen people.

If we want to speak about the first actions of God, then we must speak with the mouth and the accent of a member of the chosen people, after the manner of one who has learned to speak about God and godly things as a result of a conquest: there they knew God intimately. If therefore we want to write about the first things and if moreover we want to speak about God's part in them, then we cannot do without these words, words that remind one of the conquest; this is the way to testify about divine action. It is the same God. That is why one can say: the way he made himself known in his historical dealings with his people, when he led them into the promised land, is the same way in which he always has acted with man — in a historical manner. If one is going to testify about God from the beginning, he will have to testify about the same kind of God from the first days. If we are allowed to testify about him as a God who deals with us in a historical manner, it is as this same God that we now must proclaim him. We have to say that he was the same from the very beginning and that he made himself known to man in the same manner.

His contact with us has always been in a historical manner. He has adapted himself to the rhythm of human generations.

And so we see, at long last, after much wandering about that we have arrived at paradise, which according to common acceptance must be considered as the prototype of any paradise: the paradise of the book of Creation. We have tried to safeguard this wonderful story, and not to wrench it away from the loving care with which the holy people cherished it — to read it in the light of the vision of faith which is that people's very own. Of course, they have known stories, they have heard the fairy tales of the peoples around them. They have understood the imagery of the dreams in which cravings of long centuries are lamented in the present situation. They have known about the numerous tales in which a golden age is typified: times and places so described that death has no approach to them. But however this be, however their language has been influenced by a vocabulary which resembled the vocabulary of other peoples, one thing stood out unmistakably for them: if they are to write a story about those things, and describe the part God has played in them, then God has to be pictured after the manner of the God who liberates and leads, because that is the name he has acquired among them.

In the story of the Book of Creation we find a few sentences which can aid us considerably to see

how they strove to cope with current tales. In Gen.
2, 8 we read that God **planted** a garden in Eden and
that he put man into it. This already has a familiar
sound for us. And more familiar for us yet is the
whole climate of this paradise, when we see what
is written in verse 15 about it.

"The Lord God took the man and put him in the
garden of Eden to till it and keep it." We should not
say that these most probably are editorial words,
which are not important for the understanding of the
story. On the contrary: it is these sentences which
carry the story and make its meaning clear. They
tell us how the garden came into being and how
man happened to be found in this wondrous place
of grace. How man has been placed in a garden
full of life-giving trees, where he would not taste
death, where he would live everlastingly. We see
how the holy books describe this, and the words
have a familiar sound for us. Just for a moment
we hear the grand detail that God lays hold of
something, that he appropriates something: man.
Next, having taken him, he makes him rest in the
garden he has planted. He makes man rest in the
holy place which he has arranged, and what this
means we can very well surmise from what we have
heard before. Thinking about rest, and about the
manner in which it is expressed here, we notice that
the same word is being used here that could be used
(and in fact has been used) to describe the action
with which God transferred the Israelites to the
promised land. For the correct interpretation it is

therefore more than interesting that the story is
placed in such a frame. The story must be read with
this view in mind; this is the pattern from which
it has been cut, the reference in which it has been
framed. The way God deals with his chosen people
determines also his way of dealing with man from
the very first days. It is the same God who acts in
the same way: the way in which he has made himself known. I dare say we know by now that he
has made himself known by liberating his chosen
ones — in no other way. If we want to speak about
the same God as doing something in connection
with the first man, we shall have to make him act
in the same way.

The first man must do in regard to paradise the
same things the pious Israelite had to do as in regard to the promised land. He has to till it and to
keep it. He has to keep a law, the same way the
Israelite had to. He may not of his own account
reach for the fruit of the forbidden tree, because if
he does so he will die. He will be cut off, expelled,
as the sanction has it in numerous laws protecting
the Covenant of God's people with its Lord. In
the sanctuary of paradise man has to live according
to the divine norm, in accordance with the plans
God has for him. We all know (from our childhood
we might say) that this is where the difficulties of
paradise began. God reveals himself in a historical
action to be with man, to seek intimacy with him.
This intimacy with God can be found only if we
are prepared to subject ourselves to this relationship,

if we agree to observe the manner in which God
has deigned to meet us. We must keep to the road
which God has made for us; if not, we will never
reach the land beyond the river Jordan, the promised land. These are the consequences of the manner in which God has wanted to make himself
known; this is the way he has made our acquaint-
ance. The rules we have to keep are derived from
God's journey through history. They are the rules
and regulations of a historical covenant. This Covenant and the rules, the covenant and the laws, we
must never sever from the God who has given them,
and this God, the same yesterday, today and in all
eternity, has made himself known in the course of
history. For good reason in some old songs his name
is called, as might be translated, "The Sinai One"
(Judges 5, 5), because the road from Sinai to Zion
justifies this.

Should we wonder that the conditions imposed on
the first man in the biblical testimony are described
in the same way? The first man had to be pictured
in a situation that reminds one of the promised land,
and we have seen the part which trees and fruits
and making use of them plays there. The shade of
beneficent trees is the shade of God's protection. For
an Israelite, land denuded by locusts is incompatible
with the idea of God's presence. But we know, too,
it is a country given by God. It is not man who
made it. God led them into it with a strong arm
and amidst many wonderful signs. That is why they
say in their language that God "made man rest,"

a verbal form which is eminently suited to describe God's actions.

That is how it was in the case of the first man. God put him to rest in the divine domain and this cannot be conceived without trees. According to the way Israel experienced God, the people had to write in this particular way about man's entrance into paradise.

They are forced, if we may say so, to enlarge upon the scenery of trees and fruits, because this is the way to speak about the promised land. It is a land with trees which bear fruit, and we have already spoken about their protecting shade. One is in the promised land if one is able to enjoy the fruits of the land. But we repeat: it is a God-given land and therefore the fruits also are God-given; man may not reach out for them with impunity.

Much could be said about stories in which trees of life, and also trees of knowledge of good and evil are found. There are other peoples in the world besides the people of Israel, and this same imagery has been used many times. But that is not the chief point that concerns us. It does not matter if certain words are also used elsewhere and if others also have placed such trees in the garden of their gods. The biblical testimony wants to describe the first man after the pattern of the Israelite who enters the promised land. This is the true model which has served. In this case we also know what this means: to be allowed to eat the fruits of a

special tree. In this connection we can understand
what it means to reach out for the fruit on one's
own account, unauthorized. In doing so one does
not respect God's gifts, one overlooks that it is God
who gave paradise and its fruits to man. In this
perspective we have to interpret this tree and its
fruit. The apple blushes with pride, it is integrated
in a vast perspective. One should relish it in the
right manner. There are other instances in the holy
books where the fruit of a tree is made use of in
the same way.

We know about the prophets and we know they
must have been very close to the Lord to be able
to prophecy. They must have been intimate with
him to be able to write about divine things in the
proper way. They must, as it were, have been ad-
mitted into paradise. Could this be the reason why
God is said to put the words into their mouths?
Are they allowed to savor the words which they
are going to speak as wonderful fruits, and are they
only in this way able to explain God's intentions?
They can do so, because their mouths are filled
with God's words, because their mouths have acquired the divine accent. God fulfills his plans with
his servants, the prophets, by making his intentions
known to them. He does not withhold these from
them. God communicating his words is described
as if he puts them into the mouths of the prophet
like a fruit. And when the pious Israelite ponders
thankfully about the good things of God's law and
justice, he speaks about a fruit that has been given

him which enables him to live according to the
divine law. It is a fruit which had to be given.
In the framework of God's dealing with the Israelites this way of speaking springs forth from their
dreams about the holy land with its many trees, all
of them bearing fruit.

The verses of this second chapter of Genesis are
of great importance. They show the continuity of
the holy books. In writing about the very first
things the way they do, these verses make present
the God whom we already know from his revelation, at the beginning of human history; the very
same, historically acting God.

6

THE UNSTABLE EQUILIBRIUM

In this paradise, this blessed garden, we meet the tension which arises between God and man; it shares in the frailty of all human things. Man had been made able to be an inhabitant of this garden. But he is also able to possess this garden in a manner which has not been ordered by God. He is able to transgress the prescribed limit, not to observe the norm which God has put to him. He is able to take for himself the things which should be given to him, and by taking in this way he shatters paradise. Man is then put back into the place from which he had been taken. He is expelled, because he did not follow the road one must travel to reach divine intimacy. Cherubim must guard the entrance of paradise after this — heavenly beings, with flaming swords. Henceforth whoever wants to enter into this domain will have to be of heavenly stature. Cherubim also keep watch over the Holy of Holies. Maybe these heavenly beings force us to ponder again. We know that they had a fixed place in the temple of Jerusalem. They had to spread out their wings above the Ark, to protect the sanctuary, where only the high priest, and then only on exceptional occasions, was allowed to enter. And thus again we realize that paradise has something to do with Jerusalem. The same guardians who kept watch over the Holy of Holies also guard the sanctuary of the enclosed paradise.

From Jerusalem they have looked back into the farthest past; they have discovered a paradise, and they have testified to God at the beginning of things. They have put into words the tragedy of human possibilities. The earth mourns and withers away, because this blessed earth has been desecrated by its inhabitants; they have transgressed the laws and broken the rules. Therefore a curse devours the earth, and its inhabitants must do penance, and instead of pure fruits, of a holy vine, the earth brings forth thorns and thistles. But this consideration, this tragedy, too, has its roots in the city which was chosen by God, a city about which one could dream.

We know its tragedy: Jerusalem was burned; she was made into a smoking pile of debris; wild animals roamed about in her seeking their prey; her inhabitants were dragged away and their bereaved sobs still resound in the psalter: "Jerusalem if I forget you, let my right hand wither." What had befallen Samaria now befalls the proud capital of Judah. It is possible that the story of paradise was composed when the tragic downfall of the city loomed on the horizon during the frantic days after the fall of Samaria, when the people of Jerusalem asked themselves: "How long yet, O Lord?" They dream about their visions of the city on the mountain, but they keep their dread. Shall it last, when prophets have to lash out at the conduct of the people? Shall the city stand, if people think they are able to safeguard the safety of the city themselves, if they think they themselves are able to take the fruits of conquest, if they think they can take their lot into their own hands?

The city image of Jerusalem fades. The prophets have foretold it. At least the good prophets have. There were good prophets and false ones. The books of the Old Testament still show warning against false prophets. Whatever they do, whatever signs they are able to show, the people must never listen to them, when they encourage them to leave the God of the Covenant and to go and serve strange gods. Over against these false prophets we find the good ones. Their place is, as it were, between God and the people. They must remind them of the Covenant. And in their prophetic words they must maintain the wonderful tensions which characterize this Covenant. They must proclaim God's demands, teach the people that they have received something from God, that something has been given to them at the end of a long road. In prophetical words they must be told that they have not wrought this with their own hands, but that God's powerful hands have wrought it for them, when he led them and went before them as a consuming fire. With his scorching breath he burned a road for them. He was a curse for those who hated him. That is why they dare not take his graces with their own hands. The good prophets therefore must refuse to take the side of the wishful thinking of the people. They must refuse to sever the fulfillment of God's promises, however glorious this may have been until now, from the fulfillment of the Covenant.

And in the writings of the prophets we can see how the people in certain circumstances looked at the realization of God's promises. People tire of always restraining their expectations. They want to dissolve tension into the certainty of possession. They harden the docile hearts for which their king Solomon had prayed. They shut them up against the daily summons. They refuse to listen to the "Hear, O Israel. . . ." In their hearts the appetite for the God of the Covenant has been quenched. Their warm enthusiasm is chilled, and the hearts of the people turn to stones. The temple of stone, made by the hands of man, is their possession. The city has become the city of their own glory and strength, no longer the fruit of God's benign grace. They try to bind God down instead of adoring him, and they try to fetter him with their vulgar wishes. They put everything on their own level. They try to confine God within the space of the temple of Jerusalem. They forget they have been granted a Covenant with One who is greater than the temple.

The people found themselves prophets to put this attitude into words. They are the prophets who think that Jerusalem cannot totter in all eternity. These prophets forgot that this expectation is linked up with the grace of the Covenant, in virtue of the

agreement that God entered upon with his people
at the foot of Sinai. They leave the people in their
illusion that all is finished now, that all God's promises have been fulfilled, that they have nothing to
look forward to. They cut off their own road to
the future. They deceive the people and the sense
they impose can easily be guessed: nonsense. Mad-
men! They do away with God's fidelity as regards
the future. They teach the people to cling not to
the matchless divine fidelity, but rather to the
splendor of Jerusalem, which God gave only in
virtue of his fidelity. They think that they can cut
themselves loose from that divine faithfulness. In
this way they still hope to find protection in the
city. They swear by the temple. They shout it:
have not we got the temple, the temple, the temple?
What else can be expected from us? What else
should we need? Have we not all that God has
promised he would give? The significance of the
earthly house of God for them was confined to
earthly pursuits, it did not reach beyond the
earthly horizon. It is clear that those prophets have
not taken part in God's council. They cannot interpret God's thoughts.

At the same time there are also good prophets,
men of God, who announce the truth and the divine
reliability. Jeremiah is one of them. He knows that
God watches, that the mystery of the Covenant is
operative in him; this is what he, being a prophet,
must testify. He is convinced that the Covenant
holds good. He knows the tensions which accompany

God's promises; the realizations which are balancing on them always show a precarious equilibrium. He knows what disillusionment awaits the people if they try to measure with earthly measures the place that God chose for himself (cf. Jer. 7). He knows what will happen to the temple and to Jerusalem if the measuring rod has not been cast in heaven. Their grasp will go amiss and they will not believe their own eyes; the result will be ruins, just as of old in Shilo. And all this only because they confided in deceptive slogans and made the temple itself into a slogan. What avail will the temple be, if instead of a place of adoration it is turned into a den of thieves? They go through the motions of sacrificing there, but they follow only the movements of their hardened hearts. Jeremiah's preaching is more than a plea for inwardness and fervor; his heart cries out for sincerity, for really saying "Amen" to God's faithfulness and for trusting in his help, because their help is only in the name of the Lord. We know how it ended.

Jeremiah stands at the end of this period in the history of the Jewish people. His lamentations are one long mourning-song for the downfall of the city and its temple. The flames leaped high into the sky, the very horizon seemed to be aflame. The people start on the road of roaming. They are chased across the frontiers from which they had come. Again they are wandering, as were their fathers before God liberated them of this necessity. They could have foreseen it; they knew what the

victorious armies would do to the peoples and the
cities which they conquered. They knew the war
customs of those peoples of Mesopotamia.

That is why it seems to us that the story of paradise on the first pages of holy Scripture was written
in the period of unstable equilibrium which obtained
in Jerusalem, when Samaria had fallen, while Jerusalem, owing to an incredible converging of circumstances, i.e. the benign hand of the Lord, was
able to hold out against strong enemies, and when
the people understood the prophet who said: "All
that fight against her and her stronghold and distress her, shall be like a dream, a vision of the night."
On the occasion of such happy events the people
celebrated in jubilant songs the strength which God
had given to the city and exalted in the paradisic
waters on which their city floated forever, impregnable and perhaps prouder than any.

The beginning of things and the first paradise,
pictured as an enclosed garden, suppose this parallel,
it seems to us. In this way the people were able
to give God a name, to name him after the measure
of the holy city, of a sanctuary, of Jerusalem.

7

AFTER THE FALL OF THE CITY

1. The long advent.

Jerusalem has fallen. The vision which Isaiah dreamed has fallen apart. The last days seem to have come; the prophets hold their breath. How would they be able to prophecy, now that the city is besieged and the temple aflame? Ezekiel will remain dumb during all the time when Jerusalem is in stress and the brilliant summit of the earth is deprived of its splendor. A nightmare seems to control the country. Once the fury subsided they wondered how the world could go on and how there were people still alive, after the brilliant vision of Jerusalem had vanished.

The Israelites pray to God, and praying they mourn the downfall of their city. We know that God has not left them, that even over their place of exile the heavens were opened and prophets were allowed visions. It is the same God who consoles and promises liberation through the mouths of his servants, the prophets. Perhaps their greatest consolation was the fact that he did not leave his people and that by means of the prophets he made known to them that once again freedom would dawn behind the horizon which now is still wrapped in darkness.

It has become evident to the people of Israel that God's saving grace and final revelation do not automatically coincide with the glory of Jerusalem. Ezekiel told them that the glory of God has left Jerusalem and has turned toward the east. God is not once for all tied up with the city. He is only tied up with it, because he has made a Covenant. Moreover, the safety and impregnability of Jerusalem balances on the frail equilibrium of the Covenant. It balances on the fragile relation which God wants to have with man. If man wants to leave him, he also can leave Jerusalem. And he has done so. The holy books mention the sins of the people and its kings. They mention the idolatry which broke the Covenant, which forced God to leave Jerusalem and let the city be turned into a heap of debris. Jackals roam about in it.

Through this bitter experience it becomes clear to them what revelation really means. We have seen that what it really means is that God wants to be intimate with his people. He seeks togetherness. The people were together with him in the sanctuary of the city. Each revelation was at the same time a promise. God revealed himself as guaranteeing that a king of the house of David would sit forever on the throne. When he reveals himself he always promises, at the same time, that he will reveal himself more intimately yet, that the intimacy will be closer yet. These promises therefore never will be

lost. They hold good forever. What that intimate
revelation will be, how the enhanced intimacy with
God will be realized, how God-with-us will be in
the **real** "latter days," is a mystery for the people
who stand mourning around the ruins of the city.

They cannot pierce the darkness of the future,
just as they could not see through the haze of times
primeval. But the strong ones, who in their distress
and in their mourning for the fallen city lift up their
eyes to the Lord, keep trusting that he will save
them. They trust that he will show himself to be
God, as they have heard from their fathers. They
trust that they too shall be able again to teach their
children the holy songs, and that for the generations
to come after them the refrain will remain, that his
mercy is great and his steadfast love endures forever.
They are convinced that God remains the same forever and that they, as long as the final fulfillment
has not come, always may look for a still more intimate realization of that wonderful togetherness which
God wants to bring about with us.

We may always look forward to and participate in
a growing process, in which God wants to make us
share more deeply and more intimately in his being.
We know where this will end. Our creed has it,
that this will consist in being together with God
even in his own abode. The movement which we
are trying to describe leads us up to the very steps
of the throne of God. This is a goal which lies beyond our world. Maybe it lies further than our

surmise goes. When the holy books try to describe
it they say: God will be everything to everyone.
Everything tends to this, all endeavors along the
road which God has made for us, are directed toward it, and it is something that lies further than
our eyes at first sight can reach. It is a road that at
a given moment leaves the earth and leads into
heaven. We believe that God in that final stage of
intimacy remains his own self. He is also the one
who works this end. It is he who conducts the road
up to the very steps of his throne, and who carries
his elected along the road they travel, even after
the downfall of Jerusalem. We have seen that God
accompanies the life of his people. He has made a
road that is a road of saving grace. In the light
of this conviction the sacred authors were able to
write about that people, going back to the furthest
past, taking this road of saving grace as their measure.
It seems to us that we must say the same about
the line that goes into the future. In the future we
must mention God's name, call him by his own name
and walk into the future in the name of the Lord.

About that future we can say the same as we did
about the past: we do not know what it will be like.
It is something which is simply unknowable for us.
It escapes us, it is hidden from our eyes. But we
do look toward the future, as the chosen people
looked into the future, holding in its hands the
rich promises of God, and being carried in virtue
of these promises. They know and testify that God
does not leave them alone, that he remains with them

as he was with them of old and shall be in all
eternity.

The wonderful name by which he wants to be
called by men is the name which became known
during the exodus and conquest of his people. It
is a name which has a paradisic glamor, because
the mountains melted like wax, the enemies were
dispersed and everywhere the desert blossomed when
at the head of his people he made a road toward
the domain he had allotted them. If they want to
speak about him in the future, they must, as was
the case with their speech in the past, take into account that holy name. The speech about God's
future actions must be taken from the method of
speaking of the historical revelation, because it is
the same God who wants to be called thus. We have
seen that the people of Israel drew the line which
carried them to Jerusalem back to the very first
beginning. In the same way, we now see this line
being drawn toward the future, toward the time
when everything will be fulfilled. So too, we here
have a way of speaking that takes its measure from
the historical revelation. This is the way the Lord
has taught men to speak. In these accents they
must praise him, because their mouths are full of
God's praise. They praise him on account of his
mighty deeds. Their mouths have become used to
the taste of these praises, and this shows when they
speak about the future.

In this way they prayed for return to Jerusalem
and liberation of the holy city. The prophets describe

in daring metaphors a new exodus which will lead
from the land of exile toward a newly promised holy
land. A road of saving grace blossoms in the desert
and if they convert themselves sincerely, and if they
swear in all humility on the life of the Lord, then
it will happen again that the peoples around will
call themselves happy because of the promises
made to this people. They will again take upon
themselves the part of a mediators, a task which
God entrusted to them when he called Abraham,
their father, from the ends of the world. Then
they will remedy the misery of a lost land, reclaim
a new land, and no more have to sow in the midst
of thistles and thorns. We hear familiar sounds in
this and we know what they mean. And the river
flows on. People keep testifying about God in this
way, they ponder about their solitude, they think
about adapting it to their present situation, they
dream about it in the wilderness. From there the
voice will be heard which announces that the time
of redemption is near. We know that it is about a
revelation of God who wants to be near to us, who
wants to keep carrying human history.

2.   God-with-us.

We do not know, beforehand, how good he is,
how he wants to meet us. It will not be in the same
way that it happened before. God will not be intimate in the way of one who lives in a temple and
who has his throne in Jerusalem. God now wants
to be near us by sending us his only Son.

His Son will be man in our midst. He will be a son of the progeny of David, and his wonderful name will be indeed "God-with-us." He will be the Covenant in person. Cannot we expect everything from God, now that he has given us his own Son? This is the way God has responded to the desire of the ages. This is the word he sends. Here he intervenes. Here he comes to meet us.

The long line of human history, which he had always carried, receives now a Head, a Leader, someone who marches at the fore, sent by God. Now the one who leads is not a person endowed with heavenly powers, but is himself a heavenly being in the most absolute sense of the word, because he is God's only Son. He is sent by his Father to march at the head of humanity in the last stage which will lead to definitive intimacy with the Father. This stage will lead us where the Father wants to have us, that is, his own golden altar in heaven. In order to cross the boundary we need the help of heaven. We cannot reach there by earthly means or by starting from the earth. The road to heaven is only opened from within. That is why someone first had to descend upon this earth, before it was possible to ascend into heaven from this earth, into heaven, where the intimacy with God shall be most intense. There at long last all will be realized: God everything unto everyone. Toward this the whole course of human history leads.

In this stream Christ-Emmanuel (if we may say so) is the rapids where the stream intensifies its

course. Now it is evident, it is clear where the
course carries us. God has come out to meet us;
the people who sat in darkness have seen a great
light and in the splendor of that light we can go
on, we continue on the road that leads us onward
until we stand in God's sight. It is he who paves the
road which leads to the final fulfillment, to heaven.
Therefore he is the one who is to come and we
shall not look for another. The road he makes is
the straightway of the road which has been made
by God in virtue of the old Covenant, entered into
near mount Sinai, in Arabia. This road starts in the
desert; it has become the measure for all God's
promises; all his revelations form the last lap of this
first revelation of his name.

The line of the Old Testament reaches its peak in
St. John the Baptist. We find ourselves on the other
side of the Jordan, in the twilight between the
two Testaments. The Precursor is our guide; he
points out the road that must lead us to Jesus. With
him we march up to the boundary river of the
promised land.

Now the Precursor stands there and the evangelists, in describing him, think about the exodus;
they quote Isaiah who prophecied about a new
exodus; they have not forgotten the language which
they learned to speak. . . . So St. John's figure is a
striking one, because he is different from the shaken
reed along the river. We must go beyond him if we
wish to enter the promised land; via this summit
of the Old Testament we must go if we want to

find the footprints of Jesus. He makes the road for the one who comes after him.

Next comes the baptism of Jesus. The heavens are opened above him and the Spirit descends in a visible form. The Jordan follows its course; nothing now stops its course, as happened when Joshua entered the promised land. Another entrance is disclosed now, and a dove is visible.

St. John, the friend of the Bridegroom, rejoices greatly. He hears the jubilant voice of the Bridegroom who takes possession of his bride. He rejoices because he has been allowed to prepare the way for him. He has been allowed to conduct the Old Testament up to the threshold of the New, up to the Jordan, the frontier of the promised land, where the desert changes into the land which God has given as an inheritance to the forefathers.

In Jesus all the lines converge. He fulfills everything of the Old Testament. This makes it difficult to clarify many things which are said about him, because all the lines converge in him. He is the living intimacy which God wants to have with us. The strange thing is that we had never expected this. According to the Old Testament we have represented to ourselves the intimacy of God with his people in a manner bound up with space. One was allowed to be a member of the household of God, to have part in his friendship and in the grace which he distributed in the temple, and thus this

frail intimacy could be described as a paradise. Now
however, it appears, we have to understand it in
a "personal" way.

In Jesus the wonderful intimacy of God-with-us
takes its full shape. To put this into words, one must
again make use of the language of the Old Testament.
Most of these words have a special sound, but now
they can be used to explain the reality we find in
Jesus.

Where of old the prophet could say: "Citizen of
Jerusalem, you are the vineyard of the Lord," Jesus
now takes the place of the holy land; he goes and
stands in the place of the temple, to indicate where
one can go and meet God. That is why the three
different methods one can use in speaking about the
conquest of the holy land, as we have already
vaguely indicated, can also be discovered in what
is said about Jesus. We speak about him in this
way, we see him chiefly as the fulfiller of all God's
promises. But at the same time it is possible to
speak about him in the manner of the exodus and
the entrance into the promised land. It is also possible to surround him with all the miraculous events
of the exodus.

3.   The true bread.

Jesus' life ends in Jerusalem. His passing from
life into death marks the passing from death into life,
because in his death life is gained. He is the grain
of wheat that must fall to the earth and die in order

to bear much fruit. The ascent toward the decisive moment of his life is described in the old way. When Moses and Elijah stand in his splendor on Thabor Jesus speaks with them about his departure, his "exodus" which shall take place in Jerusalem. We know also the episode of his life when the Passover was at hand. Jesus in a miraculous way fed the multitude that followed him. They asked him for a sign, a sign from heaven, which would give evidence as the manna of old had done. This was the real bread from heaven. Which sign from heaven could Jesus show them? In the synagogue of Capharnaum Jesus points to himself as the true bread from heaven. He is the final blessing of the people, on its way to the final Passover: tangible grace of God. He supports us on our way, if we have the courage to accept him. And if we accept him, we can hear from his dying mouth the assurance that this very day we shall be with him in paradise. If we follow his footsteps, we arrive there where God wants man to be.

4. The true vine.

We see, too, in Jesus the feature of the promised land. The Messiah not only makes an abundance of wine flow on a wedding feast, so much that we can still drink from it. More than this, he himself can be considered as the true vine. The vine is the promised land.

The fruit of the land signifies the land itself and we know the promises which Joshua carried when

he returned from his reconnoitering with a bunch
of grapes. It may seem strange, but we are inclined
to say that Scripture did not mean a genuine vine
when it mentions a true vine. This may perhaps
sound improbable. But then we forget that everything, when compared with Jesus, becomes shady
and that, when his wonderful splendor shines in
this world, he, the true light and the light of the
world, places everything in a different light. Jesus
in this way is explained as the promised land, the
land of rich promises. Then too the intimacy which
we are allowed to enjoy in this promised land must
be worded in similar terms. We must be called
branches of this vine, and this indicates how intimate the relation is which we are allowed to have
with Jesus. Words of the Old Covenant are used
here in order to make us better understand a vast
new reality. Thus we remember the vineyard of
which Isaiah spoke.

But over and above this we think of the wonderful fulfillment of the Covenant which is entered
upon in Jesus' Blood during the Last Supper, as a
wonderful blessing of the fruit of the vine. Here
the Covenant reaches a peak above which we never
shall reach. After this we need expect no other; the
intimacy with Jesus, the being together with God,
God-with-us, has reached a climax, and this by
means of the signs of the land of promises. Here we
reap the fruits of all that was ever promised to the
forefathers, the fruits of the promised land — and
everybody knows how meaningful this is.

5. The son of David.

Jesus is called the Son of David. In him are fulfilled the promises which were made to the royal house of David. He is a king, but not a king by earthly standards. His kingdom is not of this world, cannot be understood in terms of this world. But we must nevertheless speak about it in making use of the rich promises of the past, in order to indicate that these promises take us further than we had thought.

The kingship of Jesus resembles the kingship of former kings. They had a function in the Covenant which God made with his people. They had a task in the conquest and safeguarding of the land. They went at the head of the people in order to show them a road, to lead them on the road that leads to salvation. They were kings in protecting the city and the temple, in keeping the Covenant. They were the keepers of the seal of God's faithfulness. It therefore is not strange that Jesus at the decisive moment of his life is called a king. When speaking with Pilate he testifies about himself. But the same thoughts suggest themselves when on the first Passion Sunday he solemnly comes down from the Mountain of Olives and ascends the slope which leads to the temple of the Lord, the house of his Father.

The people cheer him and this is described as the ritual of a crowning. "Blessed is he who comes in the name of the Lord. Even the king of Israel!"

When the evangelists write about this, it is evident that the shadow of his approaching death hovers over this scene — as does also the splendor of his nearing glory. Then the angels will receive a glorious answer to their jubilant question: "Who is the king of glory?" "He is the Lord, mighty in battle!"

6.   More than the temple is here.

Jesus is also the fulfillment of the temple. He is the real holy place which God has chosen for himself, the sanctuary in which he wills to be tangibly present among men. He is God-with-us in person, he is the Covenant, the light for the gentiles. As in old days in the dream of the vision of Jerusalem, the temple stood aglow with divine splendor.

But in Jesus God can be adored in spirit and truth. He is the newly anointed stone, anointed and corner-stone at once. The entrance into heaven is shown in his life. We know that for the Israelites the temple was the hallmark of God. In a certain tradition it became clear that the temple was the seal upon which God had impressed his promises. With this seal all his promises and their fulfillment were sealed. The temple gave the certainty of fulfillment. All this and much more holds good for Jesus. In him is conjoined all that was said about the earthly temple, made by the hands of men. We remember the vision of Ezekiel. This prophet pondered about a new temple and the Lord showed him a temple with an abundance of water. There

the fountain of all fertility and life was found, and
all glory had its origin there.

Jesus can point to himself as the fulfillment of
this vision. He brings the vision of Ezekiel to fulfillment. Streams of living water flow from within
him. His Heart is the fountain of all life and consolation. Therefore all must go up to him, up to
that sanctuary. The vision of the prophet has become true. In those days the mountains will drip
with wine and the hills flow with milk. There shall
be an abundance of water, a fountain will spring
up within the house of the Lord.

At still another time, at an important moment of
his life, we hear about a temple. It is the night of
the betrayal, in the darkness of the trial before the
Council. During that night of the trial the splendor
of Jesus' glorification is already visible. Jesus speaks
to the High Priest in the words of a resplendent
vision: The Son of man shall be seated at the right
hand of power and coming on the clouds of heaven.
In order to penetrate the darkness of this night, one
needs to see this vision anew: Jesus is accused of
wanting to destroy this earthly temple, already
built, in order to erect another not made by human
hands. By his death and resurrection Jesus shall
be the new center of adoration, the new sanctuary.
Now that he is there, the first temple has become
useless. The temple which had been made by the
hands of men can now disappear. Because it is
made by the hands of man, people are too prone,
to construe this according to a worldly pattern, to

a measure that is not sufficient if they want to know
about the length and the width and the height and
the depth of the Lord, which surpasses all understanding.

Writing about the mysteries of this night of Jesus'
death and his subsequent resurrection, the sacred
writers fondly renew the dreams of David and Solomon, the desire for a temple. Realization of these
visions becomes clear from what Jesus does. But
in wording it, they still think in terms of the temple
and the promised land: he enters into the rest that
God had prepared for him. They write about him as
entering the heavenly tabernacles. Thus he makes
secure a final and eternal redemption.

The gospels tell us about Jesus' death. At that
very moment the curtain of the temple is rent in
two, from top to bottom. The Holy of Holies is
no longer inaccessible, now that Jesus' redemption
is effected. The coincidence of these two events is
more than accidental; they belong together. In the
letter to the Hebrews (10, 20), a composition in
which one idea is wonderfully worked out, the author
writes about it in a very intense way. There he tells
how Jesus passed through the curtain of his own
flesh in order to acquire the heavenly glory; through
his own flesh he made a road into the Holy of
Holies, up to the golden throne of the Father.
Through his passion he manifested to us the very
secrets of his Father's heart. God's intentions become manifest in his words and in his work. . . .
Our eyes are opened and we see what richness we

have been called to, with what glory we will be vested.

In order to comprehend the great movement which leads from one paradise to the other, one must indeed try to speak looking back from the fulfillment. Everything is orientated toward this; in the journey of Jesus something of that movement toward the end must transpire. We see that the words have the accent of one specified center: they are the dialect of the capital Jerusalem. Interpreting things from one fulfillment they have tried to explain other fulfillments; they have looked back and they have looked into the future. This is a typical peculiarity in all scriptural speech.

8

THE END OF ALL THINGS: BACK IN PARADISE

Scripture meditates upon the beginning of all things. The authors indicate and testify about God, their Lord, as the one who is the same, yesterday and today and forever. No other gods can stand in comparison with him. He holds everything in his hands; he leads the world from beginning to end and his servants, the prophets, are initiated into his divine intentions. Common people know nothing about the goal of things that lies hidden in the dark beyond the human horizon. God manifests himself, there as ever, always in the same manner. Thus it is possible to reach out toward the far past, and the authors have not failed in this heavy task.

They can also start speaking in the same way about the future, about that which still lies in the distance, about the things still to come. But now a new aspect is visible for those who write after the coming of Christ. They are able to write about that ever increasing nearness of God, who has come so near to us that henceforth we are able to affirm that we have a Father in heaven and that this

Father has a Son, who is God-with-us in person.
The road that leads toward the end is at the same
time a road which leads to an ever approaching
nearness, an ever increasing intimacy. God remains
indeed always the same. But we approach nearer
and nearer to him; continuously it becomes clearer
what he has in store for us, and what even the angels are anxious to know.

There are many islands floating in the blue
Mediterranean. To one of them St. John was exiled.
In this exile he goes into ecstacy and describes, in
a book full of consolation and encouragement, what
is revealed to him there. He tries to picture the
glory which in the hereafter will be given to Chris-
tians, once they have escaped from this earthly
business. In order to describe this great unknown
and to testify about God's actions in that stage, he
again makes use of the old imagery. Those images
are not yet worn out, and in them is incorporated
an ever increasing reality. They contain the full
richness of that final fulfillment of God, who will
be everything to everybody. And just as was the
case in the testimony about the life of Jesus, so
also here the blessings of the exodus receive their
fulfillment: the Holy of Holies is revealed. In
Revelations we read about the glory of Jerusalem,
and the vision of paradise looms up again in its
full splendor. The consolation for the churches of
Asia Minor is the consolation of paradise; it simply
could not be otherwise.

He who conquers shall eat of the tree of life which

is in the paradise of God and he shall not be hurt by the second death. He receives some of the hidden manna which the Israelites kept in the Holy of Holies in a special vase.

Now that everything is revealed we are able to look behind the curtain and we can share in the hidden mystery of that bread which was given them on the road of life, and which supported that life on that road to the promised land. He who conquers will be made a pillar in the temple of God and he will be named in the name of the new Jerusalem of God, the new Jerusalem which comes down from heaven, and which has its origin not from this world.

The metaphors tumble over one another, they whirl about, as it were, and we wonder how St. John did not tire of speaking in so many various ways about heavenly beatitude. We find it difficult to see how at one time there is a glorious temple in the heavenly Jerusalem and at another time a temple is superfluous. It takes away our breath when in one sentence the part of the tree of life is called the part of Jerusalem. We like to call these "exuberant metaphors," and we really can say no more about it. Could it be that St. John needs all of holy Scripture's ways of speaking in order to describe the last things and the miracle that follows them? That new reality will be so rich, so full, so all-comprising and so all-fulfilling. The Old Testament pictures the nearness, the presence of God to man in the promised land with the temple as its summit. In St. John's way of speaking it becomes also the nearness of bride and bridegroom. And the intimacy which God wanted to have in the very beginning with man, and which was expressed in the metaphor of a luxuriant garden, seems also necessary to describe the final fulfillment.

As St. John sees the new heaven and the new earth, the holy city, the new Jerusalem, comes down out of heaven as a bride adorned for her husband. This city prides itself in God's glory; in this city is the river of the water of life, which flows from the throne of God and of the Lamb; in the middle of the plain, on either side of the river, as once in paradise, stands the tree of life, with its twelve kinds of fruits, yielding its fruits each month. As a consolation for those who might remember the first paradise and the curse we inherited from there, it is now said: "There shall no more be anything accursed."

This will come when the first earth and the first heaven will have vanished; when the sea, out of which the dry land came in the beginning, will no longer be there. That will be the definitive end. The evolution of mankind toward God will be fulfilled; they are with him and they are in paradise.

"The question of paradise in the holy Books is the question of a manner of speaking." According to this manner, one can happily answer this paradise question. To describe it one must use images which are typically eastern and difficult for us to understand. We have not followed this manner of speaking. We hold that the paradise story, from the very first pages of Genesis, is much more than a "manner of speaking." Truly, it is also that, but it is not the manner of speaking which is the revelation. We cannot disassociate ourselves from this manner of speaking. The paradise narrative includes more than a contrasting picture of human disappointment. It is more than just an embroidered fancy-tale, more than a value-opinion of the phenomenon "man" according to the manner of writing of some certain human culture. In Scripture this story is a magnificent testimony of the history-making action of God who entered into a Covenant with his people. It is a part of the testimony that God, from the beginning, was **the** God, the same God who revealed himself to the people of Israel in their glorious exodus from Egypt and their entry into the promised land.

Paradise is the first phase of God's saving action; it is the first point, the starting point, from which man, despite disappointment and desertion, has been able to grow toward glorious intimacy with God. In paradise the road of salvation begins which will lead to heaven, into the heavenly paradise. The difficulty seems to be that we cannot verify this. Every beginning not only is difficult: it escapes us. Hence emphasis must be placed on the manner in which God in paradise occupies himself with man, and the manner in which God wants to be God-with-us. Then we will see his powerful arm throughout history, and his leadership will take us to the very end. But as regards this future we will have to testify about his actions, and we know how: wherever he acts, the world changes; when he sends forth his Spirit the face of the earth is renewed; his action is always paradisic and must be painted in paradisic colors. The image of Jesus mirrored in the water of Cana is an abundant messianic wine, is blessing of the promised land and therefore reminiscent of paradise. But at the same time it is a promise of what is to come, because in that sign a New Covenant was made and we expect its coming.